STEPS TO
RECOVERY

Sara Miller McCune founded SAGE Publishing in 1965 to support the dissemination of usable knowledge and educate a global community. SAGE publishes more than 1000 journals and over 800 new books each year, spanning a wide range of subject areas. Our growing selection of library products includes archives, data, case studies and video. SAGE remains majority owned by our founder and after her lifetime will become owned by a charitable trust that secures the company's continued independence.

Los Angeles | London | New Delhi | Singapore | Washington DC | Melbourne

STEPS TO
RECOVERY

A CLINICIAN'S GUIDE

GRAEME FLAHERTY-JONES and SARAH DEXTER-SMITH

Los Angeles | London | New Delhi
Singapore | Washington DC | Melbourne

Los Angeles | London | New Delhi
Singapore | Washington DC | Melbourne

SAGE Publications Ltd
1 Oliver's Yard
55 City Road
London EC1Y 1SP

SAGE Publications Inc.
2455 Teller Road
Thousand Oaks, California 91320

SAGE Publications India Pvt Ltd
B 1/I 1 Mohan Cooperative Industrial Area
Mathura Road
New Delhi 110 044

SAGE Publications Asia-Pacific Pte Ltd
3 Church Street
#10-04 Samsung Hub
Singapore 049483

Editor: Susannah Trefgarne
Assistant editor: Talulah Hall
Production editor: Rachel Burrows
Copyeditor: Jo North
Proofreader: Jo North
Indexer: Silvia Benvenuto
Marketing manager: Samantha Glorioso
Cover design: Naomi Robinson
Typeset by: C&M Digitals (P) Ltd, Chennai, India
Printed in the UK

Library of Congress Control Number: 2019939803

British Library Cataloguing in Publication data

A catalogue record for this book is available from the British Library

ISBN 978-1-5264-5904-6
ISBN 978-1-5264-5905-3 (pbk)

At SAGE we take sustainability seriously. Most of our products are printed in the UK using responsibly sourced papers and boards. When we print overseas we ensure sustainable papers are used as measured by the PREPS grading system. We undertake an annual audit to monitor our sustainability.

For Claire, Elliott and Matilda, thank you for all that you are and all that you have made me. To my parents, thank you for paving the way with love, kindness and opportunity. When others believe in us, we learn to believe in ourselves. (G. M. F-J)

Of all the hands life has dealt me so far I'm most grateful for some of the people in it. Those who have quietly assumed I 'can' and, when I hesitated, given me a (sometimes not so small) friendly shove. Family, friends, mentors, colleagues, and teachers, who make me laugh, make me think, and are where I feel I belong. (S. D-S)

Contents

"Whenever we talk about ourselves we tell stories. Without these stories, our experiences would sit – unconnected – like a thousand tiny beads. (Lucy Waddington)

Often the key part of the journey from chaos to clarity is telling the story. Stories give us a handle on how we feel and an ability to tolerate and accept those feelings. (Tanya Byron: *The Skeleton Cupboard*)"

About the Authors

Graeme Flaherty-Jones is a Consultant Clinical Psychologist with a passion for making psychological concepts accessible and meaningful to bring about change. This philosophy can be seen across his work as a clinician, lecturer, author, and director. Within the NHS and independent sector, he supports individuals with complex mental health and neurological conditions, combining compassion and empowerment to help people achieve their goals.

Sarah Dexter-Smith is a Consultant Clinical Psychologist and coach who has worked in a variety of physical and mental health settings. She has spent her time in work looking at how to make the broadest use of psychological thinking for all the people who use, and work in, mental health services. She is now Director of Therapies in TEWV NHS FT and enjoying working with people from other professional, therapeutic, and spiritual backgrounds.

Acknowledgements

Only with the support of many important people, were we able to bring the Steps to Recovery framework to life in the pages of this book. To those who helped in the development, piloting and refining of the Steps to Recovery framework (Laura Eggleton, Laura Jayne-Carter, Geoff Hill, Tracey Hawkins, Karen Peat and Lindsay Hill to name but a few), we are grateful for everything you have contributed. To those who have offered kind and constructive advice along the way: Sally Smith, Natasha Lord, Gemma Graham and Talulah Hall, you have all been a guiding light.

Our Trust (Tees Esk and Wear Valleys NHS FT) has been supportive and prepared to take the chance to try something different. It's given us the time to develop and evaluate the group and trusted us to find a new way of working with people. From TEWV NHS FT, Shaun Mayo, David Brown, Ruth Briel and Colin Martin have been particularly supportive at various stages of this work. Most importantly, thank you to all the individuals who have been part of the Steps to Recovery sessions and taught us the true meaning of recovery.

Online Resources

To help you work through the Steps to Recovery programme you have access to 13 worksheets to use with the person you're working with and 8 crib sheets help keep you on track in each session.

Visit **https://resources.sagepub.com/stepstorecovery** to view and download the resources as you need them.

Introduction

Ask any individual who works in or around mental health services if they are recovery orientated in their practice and you will, hopefully, almost always get the same answer … 'yes'. However, trying to explain what this looks like in practice can be like trying to explain the 'offside rule' in football; you may know what it is, but it's hard to articulate! Trying to bring clarity to such a broad philosophical concept shouldn't be easy; otherwise it very quickly becomes reductive and loses its essence. It's also important to support recovery in different ways for different people. Yet, without any guidance, it can be tricky to forge a path that holds on to the principles of the recovery philosophy. To ensure that recovery orientated practice remains true to its philosophical roots, it can be useful to have a backdrop for conversations between you and the person you are working with, to help them find their unique recovery story. This is where the Steps to Recovery framework comes in.

How we got here

This book has been some time in the making. It established its roots a few years ago when we and many other people were thinking through how the services we worked in could embody the ideas of the emerging recovery philosophy. One of the inherent tensions has always been how we could help others become more recovery orientated, without then destroying the very essence of individual, person- (not service-) led recovery, by 'over professionalising' it. As recovery training started to become available within our NHS Trust, we could see that staff were engaged with the concepts, but there wasn't a lot of evidence of it changing people's practice. Rome (or a recovery orientated culture) wasn't built in a day, but our colleagues were telling us loud and clear that it helps to have some drawings to work from. The Steps to Recovery framework emerged to provide just that. Leaving it to chance that staff would 'get it' and start to have more recovery focused, co-produced conversations seemed tenuous.

So we set out to provide *just* enough structure to help staff bridge that gap from their previous practice to this new more fluid concept of what being 'well' meant for each person.

How to use the book

Our aim with this book, as it was with the groups on which it is built, is to offer a framework to help people consider what recovery could look like for them and them alone. As with any map there can be a number of routes from where the person is, to where they want to be and it can help to have someone along for the ride to support, without taking over. The overarching aim is to help the person develop their own recovery ladder that they can refer back to and share with others if they wish. Each session has a series of exercises for you to complete together, which will then give the person information to add to their recovery ladder. It's up to them what they do and don't include from your discussions.

The sessions follow the structure that we evaluated in our Trust. That structure was particularly important in a group setting in order to maintain some group cohesion and shared purpose to the session, but when you are working 1:1 with a person it doesn't matter what order they build their ladder in. If your conversation is naturally leading you to start with the content in session 3 for example, just follow that! Move back and forward as needed; one area of the ladder might have initially seemed clear, but the person might want to amend it after working through material in another session.

In order for you to move fluidly between the sessions themes as and when they are brought up by the person you are supporting, Table 0.1 provides a brief summary of what will be explored in each chapter. This table may be one to bookmark, as in our experience, the more familiar you are with the sessions that will be covered, the more at ease you will be 'going with' the conversation that the person brings.

Table 0.1   Session summaries

Session 1:   What is Recovery? Creating the Landscape

Explores how to introduce the concept of 'recovery' in the context of mental health and how to introduce the Steps to Recovery ladder. It ends with guided conversations on realistic goal setting and a task for the next session.

Session 2:   Who am I? Connecting with Identity

Looks at how we can help people to separate their identity from their mental health problem. The session provides conversation tips on how to strengthen a person's sense of self-identity, before looking at how to name the problem.

Session 3:   Understanding Mental Health: Perceptions, Stigma and Myths

Focuses on understanding, from a broad perspective, what is meant by 'mental health', the cultural ideas that surround the way it is perceived, and the specific things that affect the mental health of the person you are working with.

Session 4: Hope and Recovery

Explores ways in which you can help to foster hope for a person's recovery, so that they may believe that recovery is possible.

Session 5: Harnessing Skills and Resources: Doing Something Different

Focuses on helping the person to identify the skills and personal resources that they possess that might assist them in their recovery. It then introduces ways of helping the person to 'do something different' as part of their recovery.

Session 6: Developing and Maintaining Relationships

Explores the important role that relationships can play in a person's recovery. Relationships that are important to the person, what they can do to develop or maintain them and overcoming possible barriers to forming relationships are explored.

Session 7: Returning to Recovery

Explores the ways in which the person may identify signs that they are experiencing difficulties in their recovery and the things that they and others can do which might be helpful.

Session 8: Witnesses to Recovery

Introduces the role of other people in noticing and strengthening the recovery story that the person has been developing. It provides ideas for doing this in a way that supports everyone involved.

Session 9: Evaluating the Recovery Journey

Explores the tricky issue of evaluating such a personal and idiosyncratic process. Potential ways of approaching it with each person as well as ideas for navigating organisational issues are discussed.

Outline to the sessions

Each session starts with a very brief summary of what will be covered and some background as to why that area/topic may be considered important to people's recovery. It then goes through some exercises that can be discussed with the person to help them build up their own resources.

IN THE SESSION ...

You will notice that throughout the sessions, prompt questions and statements to read out are highlighted and written in separate boxes in order to help you identify them at a glance.

Worksheets to support certain exercises are referenced in the text alongside examples of completed exercise sheets. These worksheets are also available for download on the accompanying website to this book, so that they can be printed off for you to have to hand within the sessions.

Recovery Ladder

The unique aspects that make up who I am:	Witnesses to my recovery:	These people are important to my recovery:
	When things wobble I can:	Barriers – things that can get in the way:
	The changes I've already made:	
	The skills I have and things I can draw on:	I can do the following to maintain these relationships:
	These things give me hope that I can recover:	

These things can make me feel worse/how I can deal with them:

Figure 0.1   Recovery ladder

Each session ends by suggesting that you encourage the person to add the things that they have found helpful to their ladder. This is the tool that they will take away with them and is theirs to work on. In our own experience, doing this in the moment means that they capture those 'gems' and helpful reflections that can get lost if you leave it until next time. It also makes it much easier to reconnect with the work if you have the material from the last session to hand. Blank copies of the Steps to Recovery ladder (Figure 0.1) are also available for download on the accompanying website to this book, but feel free to get creative and let the person devise their own versions of the ladder at the end of each session if this feels right for them.

Each session concludes with James' story to provide an anchor for how the materials played out for one individual. This gives us space to talk about times when we adapted material or if things didn't flow quite as expected. It also helps to show what parts of the Steps to Recovery framework really mattered to James. The experiences of other people are also dotted through the book such as 'JR' and where it seems relevant we've also reflected on our own experiences.

Resources needed for each session

Worksheets have been developed where we think that a conversation can benefit from a bit of structure or where there may be useful questions to ask within the session to stimulate creative recovery conversations. Some of these worksheets have also been developed to help facilitate conversations around difficult content, where having an external prompt can take the focus off you both slightly. We recommend that you download and print the worksheets for the whole course before you start, so that you can eas-

We both love a drawing, diagram or picture. We've found that putting things on paper helps us and the other person to make sure we both understand things. It gives a different perspective seeing it drawn out rather than just being talked about. And there's something about both being able to look at a sheet that reduces the intensity of some 'tricky' conversations.

ily bring the materials into the conversation without scrabbling around with the book. There aren't many other resources that you need. If there are, then we flag that up at the start of the session.

How to get the best out of the book

If you become familiar with the materials then you will be confident to use them in whatever way suits the work you are doing together. This means you can work flexibly at the individual's pace. It also means that when topics come up that are 'out of sync' with the session structure and fit better with a later topic, you can easily make that link and start to build up the overarching understanding of the process (remember this is not a start and finish journey, it's ongoing and moves back and forth).

Note of caution

If you have not read all the sessions (even skimming them) you may miss the opportunity to make reference to other elements when it feels right to the person.

This isn't a race, nor is it a set of instructions. Don't feel you have to work from one session to the other regardless of what is useful. You also don't have to complete one session per '50 minute session' – it's not an exam or assignment!

It's also not a tool to make you feel powerful and competent, while the other person is given information and knowledge when it suits you. It might be really helpful for them to read the book and decide for themselves what is most relevant. The more you can talk about and reduce the impact of power in the conversation, the more useful it is likely to be.

We've found that it's worth keeping our own log of the journey that you're both on. This might be your reflections about your own wellbeing. It might also be small things that you've noticed about the other person as they begin to change how they talk about themselves, other people, how they dress, the way they greet you or develop the confidence in you to enable them to take more control of the session. They matter if they are linked to what you're both working on. Just be careful not to over-interpret things that are not relevant to the person. The key is always to keep talking with them about what matters to them. You obviously need to record anything significant in your formal notes, but there is usually a more subtle personal journey that you can share.

Why recovery and Narrative Therapy?

Don't take our word for it!

'In the Steps to Recovery group setting we always noted things such as someone wearing makeup for the first time or saying something different. ... I felt it was important to notice the little things that had changed that may have been slightly hidden in the conversation from the previous weeks.' (Karen, nurse)

We are long-term advocates of Narrative Therapy work, which considers the stories (narratives) that we tell about ourselves and the stories that others tell about us. These narratives can be incredibly powerful and hard to break free from and may well be so ingrained in how we and others talk about us that they feel as if they are facts. However, they can also be reshaped and we can find ways of taking more control of them than can initially seem possible.

As such, we recognise the importance of personal stories that individuals create for themselves and are 'given' by others, in shaping an individual's understanding of recovery. Within our recovery orientated practice we found that narrative theory could help us to start off conversations about 'individual meaning', the impact on individuals of 'social stories' about what being well means, and the impact of society on how individuals are able to experience and maintain mental wellbeing. In merging principles of recovery and Narrative Therapy, we wanted to develop a framework that was about being human (not ill or well) and the importance of the society in which we live.

Figure 0.2 illustrates how many of the recovery principles closely align and overlap with the philosophy of Narrative Therapy.

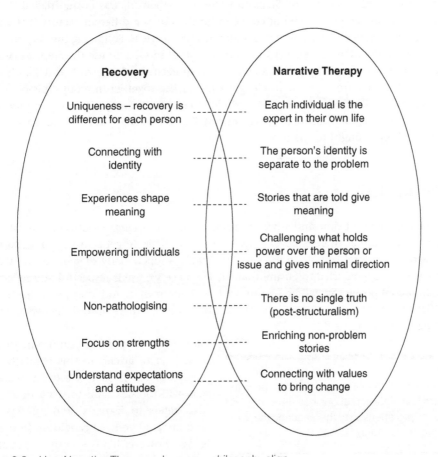

Figure 0.2   How Narrative Theory and recovery philosophy align

Narrative Therapy helped us to think about that balance between the significant influences that the society in which people live has, alongside supporting people to shape their own recovery stories. We have found that the narratives people have for their recovery can offer new hope, alter identities (spoken and hidden), and create new powerful meaning.

However, in order to empower people to create these recovery narratives, it's often helpful to first explore with them some of the implicit 'hidden' narratives (stories) that they may hold around their mental health. In our experience, recovery and narrative frameworks sit comfortably alongside each other and the core principles of Narrative Therapy inherently support the CHIME factors of recovery: Connectedness, Hope, Identity, Meaning and Empowerment (Leamy, Bird, Le Boutillier, Williams, & Slade 2011).

In blending the kind and unassuming elements of narrative work with the empowering trusting essence of recovery, the Steps to Recovery framework was born. Trialled first as a group to support people in having conversations about the different factors that support wellbeing and recovery, it was piloted in older people's services. Following the very encouraging feedback and outcomes, we began to support other services to use the Steps to Recovery material. All those people helped shape the Steps to Recovery framework as it stands today. We've had feedback from people of all ages who worked together in groups, people who've used the materials in 1:1 settings, and a whole range of staff groups in our own service and beyond. It's been a real pleasure to see the material grow and adapt as the experience of other people has been brought to the process.

Language

We took quite a bit of time and advice to think about the language that we use in the book. We've concluded that there is never a perfect turn of phrase to get across a particular point. Language is often problematic in the very fact that it is superficially shared, but individually experienced. We have tried to ensure that the language we use is respectful and reflects our thoughts about people. So, where we can, we talk about 'people' and 'they'; we hope that this is sufficiently neutral, but also refers to the personal journey that you and the person you are working with are on.

It is worth taking time to listen to yourself; perhaps even record some conversations you have at home or in work and pay attention to the language that slips in without you necessarily realising it.

Similarly, the language you use matters. We have had to attend to this regularly when applying the Steps to Recovery work and you will too. It's hard to work in a culture that refers to 'experts' and 'professionals' and not find yourself caught up in that language, however inadvertently. It can also be reassuring to slip back into those comforting words that imply some level of competence, especially when we are accompanying someone on a journey that initially has no clear end, let alone a route to follow. Words that we have had to watch include: helping, doing, shaping and telling; all well-meant, but ultimately about power and powerlessness.

We have deliberately kept the tone of the book informal and there is not a lot of reference to statistics and literature etc. This is not an academic textbook. There are other notable books on the more theoretical and philosophical components of recovery and Narrative Therapy and we are not trying to repeat that here. Where we have drawn upon particularly helpful literature, we have put the references at the end of each session.

Modelling the way

Perhaps one of the most central and important principles of 'recovery', is that it applies to everyone. Each individual can experience recovery from mental health difficulties and times of stress, but no two individuals' recovery journeys will be the same. We have always tried hard to model this approach in our practice and when using the Steps to Recovery framework we have found that sharing elements of our own recovery ladders with the people we are working with

We acknowledge that some readers may find the idea of 'open sharing' a little uncomfortable. Some clinicians find it helpful to share certain aspects of their own recovery ladder, but to mindfully leave other more personal factors back. To guide this decision making, perhaps consider 'Would it be appropriate for the person I am working with to know this about me ...?'

can be very helpful. We think it's important for everyone to take time to think about what makes their experience of life more or less positive and to think about what works best for them when things are difficult. We refer back to this throughout the book, but it's worth saying now: Don't treat this like a manual to learn in order to then 'help others'. Immerse yourself in it and use it yourself first.

We suggest that you share your own recovery ladder in session 1 as part of introducing the person to the recovery ladder template. Therefore, you will need to have completed your own ladder before this time. There is no 'right' way of completing your own ladder, but in the spirit of the Steps to Recovery framework, you may find it helpful to go through each of the session tasks with someone you trust. We have completed various pieces of recovery work ourselves and have, at different times, been supported by colleagues and family or friends in developing these. You will find a blank copy of the recovery ladder available to download on the accompanying website to this book. So now may be a good time to visit the website, print off a copy and keep it to hand as you read on.

Outcomes

No one has to 'recover' to feel that the conversations you've had have been worthwhile. The word recovery itself might even be a word that one of you doesn't like. Talk to each other about what they hope for, what would be enough, how they may express if they feel the need to stop, and how you will work together to have the best chance of meaningful change that can be sustained.

That said, people do like to know for themselves whether they've made any progress. It can also be hard to hold on to how far you've come and tempting to look only at what's left that you still want to change. If the story the person tells about who they are and what they might become/do has changed, then for us that is a great outcome. But you might have to be part of spotting that change in language and reflecting on it together. For us, the whole essence of recovery is that something that the person was bothered about has changed. Capturing this is more complex than just 'administering' a questionnaire, but well worth it. Talk about whether they can describe what a new future would look like, have they experienced that before, and be wary of it being idealistic. You might use analogue scales, or pictures or symbols to represent low and high anchor points, but do this carefully and only use symbols etc. that matter to them, otherwise this can seem patronising.

You may well work in a service that has a multitude of 'patient reported', 'clinician reported' outcome and experience measures. If you choose to complete them then try to ensure that you think about the items meaningfully and relate them to what matters to that person.

In terms of formal outcomes for the Steps to Recovery framework that guides this book, the detailed statistics are in the Appendix. These came from running the framework in a group setting over eight sessions of 90 minutes each. Our initial evaluation of the framework showed that over 90% of people who took part reported an improvement in their wellbeing and recovery scores. And 100% of people evaluated the group as having a positive effect on their recovery. We then did a more detailed evaluation across a number of services, age groups, and facilitators (Flaherty-Jones, Carne, & Dexter-Smith, 2015). There was a significant sizeable improvement on measures of both wellbeing and recovery, regardless of where the groups ran and who facilitated them.

The people in this book

Don't take our word for it!

'[The facilitator] plants the seed at the start of the sessions, the structure waters it consistently. The structure nudges you to dare to do something different.' (Molly, who worked through the framework)

We share our own experiences and those of other people throughout the book. We want to share the experiences of our clients and our own joy and frustrations in working through this process with people. James and JR were kind enough to allow us to use some of their story in more detail. In other cases, to maintain anonymity, we have combined elements of the experience of a number of people. We have loved working with them and we hope that you find something in their stories that you can connect with.

Who we are

At our core, we both share a passion for helping others to find their own meaning and path to exciting futures. This tends to find its way to expression in all that we do, be it working with a person during 'therapy', coaching a colleague in their career development, or nurturing our children's passions and interests. As clinical psychologists we recognise that people's lives are shaped by their experiences and that considering the many aspects of this can often be a helpful channel to bring about change. We like to think of ourselves as non-biased in our appreciation of theory and models, as we recognise that each can be helpful (or not) to different people in different contexts. We are also (you will be glad to hear) human and try to bring a sense of humanity when working with others. It is for this reason that throughout the book you will see elements from our own recovery ladders. In keeping with the philosophy of recovery, we hope that this in some way models that appropriately sharing our own recovery ladders can empower others to feel safe in finding theirs too.

James

We initially met James while he was being supported in one of our wards. His wife had died a year before and, while he had coped well in the first year, the impact of his grief had (it felt) suddenly overwhelmed him and he had tried to end his life. At the point he started talking with us he was bored on the ward and very restless to be home, but his family and the team were concerned about whether there was still a high risk that he would not cope with the emotions of being at home again. It was that classic dilemma. No one could say for sure that this wouldn't happen, but it was also clear that being 'stuck' on the ward was starting to make things worse. The drive to be 'doing', to be 'better', to not 'be stuck', and to be 'contributing' were themes that recurred throughout our work, both at times when they were extremely useful to James and at those times where they threatened to derail his progress. He began sessions with one of us on the ward and then once he went home, began to use the Steps to Recovery material with the other. We have both learnt a lot from being allowed to sit alongside James as he worked through a new way of balancing his strengths and carved out a new chapter of his life with his family.

JR

JR is another person that we have had the great pleasure of supporting in their recovery journey, which has taken many twists and turns along the way. JR has always been a caring and compassionate individual who, with the help of their partner, cared for their two children who sadly passed away within 18 months of each other from muscular dystrophy. Doing for others and being strong for the children was a core part of life for JR, but with such a monumental loss and with their own physical health problems emerging, a 'dark mist' of depression started to take hold. This wasn't the first time the dark mist of depression had come into JR's life, but this time it seemed to be all consuming and at times left them feeling that they could not carry on with life. JR worked with one of us using the Steps to Recovery work in both hospital and community (their own home) settings. As is the case for so many individuals, JR would at times describe taking 'one step forward and two steps back' in their recovery journey, when life threw challenges their way. At such times, the session on 'hope for recovery' was particularly important to JR and conversations around building and maintaining relationships had a very significant part in their recovery journey. It has been a privilege to share in JR's recovery story and we hope that the examples they have kindly provided in the book highlight how the different elements of the Steps to Recovery framework can have utility in different circumstances.

The book describes a way of helping to find an individual path to recovery. It has helped many people and we hope that it helps you and the people you support. Have fun with it; we hope you find it useful. Most importantly, use it in a way that suits you and the person you are working with, so that you have conversations that matter and help make a positive change.

> Until we are able to use our own words to tell our own stories, the context we find ourselves in ... says our stories for us, and usually gets it wrong ...
>
> When he proclaimed: 'You have a mental illness.'
>
> I responded: 'I thought I had a story to tell.'
>
> Beth Filson in Russo & Sweeney (2016)

Session 1

What is Recovery? Creating the Landscape

This session explores how to introduce the concept of 'recovery' in the context of mental health to the person you are working with. We look at how to introduce the steps to recovery ladder, and explain its purpose and use across the sessions. The session ends with guided conversations on realistic goal setting and a task for the next session.

For this session you will need

- Worksheet 1.1 The Recovery Ladder

Visit https://resources.sagepub.com/stepstorecovery to download

Other resources for you to refer to:

- Figure 1.1 Recovery is …
- Figure 1.2 Recovery: how we might imagine it *should* be versus how it often *is*
- Table 1.1 'Away From' and 'Towards' goals

Introducing the concept of recovery

This session provides a framework for you to talk with the person about what recovery means to them and how they imagine life might be in their preferred future.

Before you start working through this session with someone else, take some time to really think about the idea of recovery and your own assumptions and beliefs about it. Work through the questions yourself. We honestly think that until you've done that you can't effectively work with another person thoughtfully and know what you are bringing to the conversation that might not be helpful.

The session structure is a guide. Some of our conversations about recovery have been quite quick. But sometimes, they can take much longer. One of us spent nearly a whole session talking about what recovery might mean and look like. And it was time well spent. As you talk about potential hoped-for futures, make sure not to overwhelm people with what 100% would look like. Early on in a person's recovery it can be hard to trust any progress they have already made (or that other people have seen) and so aiming too high too quickly (if it's steered by you rather than them) can feel like too big an ask.

The meaning of recovery

This is one of the quotes that we have found most helpful in our conversations:

> Recovery is ... a deeply personal, unique process of changing one's attitudes, values, feelings, goals, skills, and/or roles. It is a way of living a satisfying, hopeful and contributing life even within the limitations caused by illness. Recovery involves the development of new meaning and purpose in one's life as one grows beyond the catastrophic effects of mental illness. (Anthony, 1993)

IN THE SESSION ...

Explain to the person that you have one definition of recovery that you would like to share with them (the quote in the text).

- Ask them to think about how it maps onto their own expectations, hopes and fears.
- Does any of it surprise them?
- There are many others – would it be helpful to explore some of them together or outside of the session?
- Encourage them to make some notes about what stands out for them when they think about their own recovery from where they are now.

For us, this quote covers all the elements that we would want to bring into any conversation about the future that someone wants to live. There are some elements of it that are less comfortable for us but that discomfort is precisely why it is potentially useful. A meaningful conversation should allow you to look at areas of disagreement that the person may be experiencing with family, friends or people in the health or social care system. The purpose of this session is to help the person to develop a way of bridging that gap between now and the future and between different views of recovery.

The quote above has a number of chunks of information in it, so don't skim over it in a rush to 'get on' with the next exercise. Take some time to think about which bit holds the most meaning for the person you are with. This is one of the points in the process where it can really help to have completed your own ladder and worked through the exercises yourself – you will be able to have much more fluent conversations if you have also thought about your own reactions to the quote.

Some people won't identify with the term 'illness' or will have been given a diagnosis

It's a great quote but don't be afraid to break it down and make it work for the person themselves. One person we worked with just looked blank when he saw it. But he came alive when we looked at a couple of the elements: that recovery was something that was personal to him (not ours or his family's version of it) and that he could live a life that contributed something he valued.

As you might expect, given that we've based this on narrative work, we believe that language is profoundly important. Working out the terminology that works for the person really matters. For one of us, the word recovery doesn't feel right. But 'a life that I'm enjoying' sets off a very easy conversation about what that means to me, how it feels, what I need to do to maintain that and how others contribute to it. It also gives me the space to accept and be okay with the fact that, in that life, there are times that are a bit rubbish. It's the overall balance that matters to me.

that does not sit easily with them. Remember that recovery is about *them* finding meaning in a way that enables them to live a life they want to live. That may or may not include the reduction of 'symptoms' or agreement with a diagnostic label that they've been given. Conversely some people will find a diagnosis supportive and meaningful and may well align themselves with more than one. The benefit of taking the approach outlined in this book is that the type and number of diagnoses that the person might have been given, do not make the framework any more or less potentially helpful. What's more important is a sense of curiosity that there might be a different way of working through things and a relationship (with you) that is safe enough to explore that in order to come to their own conclusions. The language that people use might also change as they progress through their journey. Stay alert to this and use the language that the person brings with them.

One of the issues we have quite frequently come across is that the very nature of the concept of recovery, i.e. that it is unique to each individual and multi-layered, can make it difficult to start a conversation. And when a person is distressed and seeking help, it can seem impossible to imagine getting from where they are to a life that is personally meaningful and fulfilling. Even daring to hope, a central tenet of recovery, can feel threatening. Figure 1.1 breaks the quote down and might help you have this conversation.

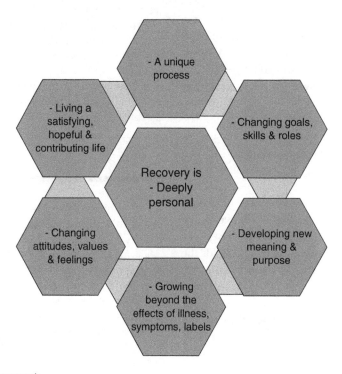

Figure 1.1   Recovery is…

There are many ways to ask about what recovery can look like to the individual. Some people can give vivid descriptions of what will be different; others can give an indication using scales e.g. 1–10 of where they are, have been and want to be. Others are very cautious and struggle to describe out loud what recovery would mean to them. They may be frightened of tempting fate, feel 'unworthy' of recovery, or be too traumatised to remember or imagine what life might *be* like rather than what it has recently been.

The process of recovery

As well as the *meaning* of recovery, the *process* of recovery is worth time for a conversation. We have often spoken with people (and fallen into the trap ourselves) who assume that other people have a life that is smooth and 'recover' from any problems they do experience in a nice steady way that leads them onwards and upwards. In reality though we all wobble around a bit and have ups and downs. Recovery is not a thing that 'happens' and is then 'done'. Getting to a more meaningful way of life can be characterised by a fleeting sense of optimism and sometimes rapid sensation of not being able to trust that progress. The graph in Figure 1.2 shows how we've talked with people about a more realistic path to recovery.

It's not an end point, it's a process that we're all engaged with every day.

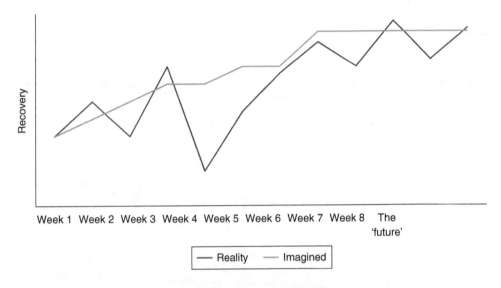

Figure 1.2   Recovery: how we might imagine it *should* be and how it often *is*

JR's Story

After coming into hospital for support with feelings of low mood and hopelessness, JR started to engage in conversations about their recovery using the Steps to Recovery framework. After just a few sessions and a short time in hospital, JR commented on how their mood seemed to have improved quite considerably from the time they entered hospital. JR had also observed 'other patients on the ward moving on' and started to think about the next step for their recovery. Wanting to build on this positive change and with a fear of becoming 'dependent on others', they decided to quickly progress their discharge back to their own home.

When meeting with JR in the week following their discharge, it was clear that something had changed. JR appeared to be quite self-critical of not having had the motivation to 'do more' since returning home. This opened up an opportunity to consider JR's perception of what their recovery might or 'should' look like. JR made reference to seeing others on the ward move 'to discharge' more

(Continued)

(Continued)

quickly than them. Having noticed a quick positive change in their own mood, they had thought that their own progress would continue to be steady. Using the graph in Figure 1.2, we discussed how, for most people, the recovery process can have many 'ups and downs', where change can occur daily or even hourly. This resonated with JR and naming it felt important. At the end of the session JR noted 'I need to give myself a bit of a break on the days when I'm having a dip in that graph', which led to a conversation around the benefit of being compassionate towards one's self during the process of recovery. We also took the opportunity to add 'self-critical thinking' to JR's recovery ladder as a sign of when things may be going less well in their recovery.

IN THE SESSION ...

Ask the person you are working with to think about this question and make a few notes: 'What does recovery mean to you?'

If they can imagine that they are living a life that is characterised by the CHIME factors: Connectedness, Hope, Identity, Meaning and Empowerment:

- How does life look? How do they feel? What are they doing? Who is there with them?
- If they need to make some changes in order to get to that experience of life, what would be different?

  - Ask them to write down things they would be excited about being different rather than things they would hope to leave behind (they will be more motivated to keep working towards positive things than away from things that worry or frighten them).
  - Think of small daily changes that they or someone else would notice.

Ask them to look at the quote again.

- Does any of it surprise them?
- Invite them to make some notes about what stands out for them.

As with any therapeutic work, listen to the meaning. For James, the man whose story runs through the book, the concrete goals – 'get out on my bike, go out in the caravan, see my friends more' – would have technically been right and totally missed the point. Underlying all of it was a desire to see people, have some hobbies again that 'created' something that he could see (it was the hobbies that both generated the social contact and produced tangible things he could see), do things that gave life a purpose (the use of the caravan was related to voluntary work not just to 'see the world'), and reconnect with people who had valued him and his family as well as making new friends.

Talking to the people around you about recovery

One of the stumbling blocks in moving towards a recovery orientated understanding of mental distress can be the understanding that other people bring to the situation. As the Steps to Recovery framework is based heavily on a narrative approach to the way we make sense of the world. So, just as you and the person you are working with will have a strong narrative (story) about how the situation has developed and therefore the 'best' way out of it, so will the people around you both. And those stories might be entirely at odds with the recovery philosophy.

We have often worked with people who will observe that their family are struggling to trust that recovery is possible, because they are still in 'shock' from what has recently happened. The conversation about recovery can often hinge on this concept of trust and the person themselves may well feel unable to trust that this is possible.

It is worth thinking about this yourself before you get into a conversation with the other person about their own recovery. It may be that you work within a framework that is heavily influenced by models of medicine, diagnosis and treatment by 'experts'. It is likely that at some point you are also going to come across colleagues who, despite the national shift in the philosophy of mental health care, have not wholly bought into these concepts themselves. And they might be the same person that you are both going to need to talk to at some point.

IN THE SESSION ...

It is worth spending some time together thinking about:

* How would they describe the nature of the relationships they have with the people who will be important through this experience?
* Who will find conversations about recovery the easiest or most difficult to think about with you both?
* Who could they call on to help them speak about recovery with those that will find the concept hard to understand?
* Who do they not want to have a conversation about recovery with at the moment?

Later we will talk about identifying a key person who can actively notice the person's recovery and, in doing so, strengthen the new story they have created about themselves; one that is more hopeful and meaningful.

The recovery ladder

IN THE SESSION ...

Have a look together at Worksheet 1.1 The Recovery Ladder.

The various sessions will help you work together to populate the person's own recovery ladder. Each step on the ladder relates to a part of life that has been shown to help individuals in their recovery. Once it's completed, the ladder also acts as a great reminder of what was important in the process; what mattered, what helped, and what they want to take forward into the future. It's very easy for the person to forget how much work they've done to shape their own recovery and the ladder can therefore act as a quick reference point.

Other people will also see snapshots of small changes that the person themselves doesn't notice (e.g. in their face, dress, speech, or what they talk about). It's helpful that they notice it and a great source of information to add into the ladder. So notice things yourself, watch for comments that other people have made and encourage the person to capture them in the ladder. But don't get into a 'battle' about whose perception is most valid if there is disagreement e.g. if the person and you disagree with the wording, they are both useful pieces of information, but it's their ladder and their story.

Realistic goal setting

Don't take our word for it

'Just seeing it written down on the paper showed me that it all made sense and made me start to believe I could do it – it was the first time I'd let myself believe it was possible.' (James)

It's deceptively hard to set goals well. We've learnt how poor we are at it and how, when we realise at some level that we are struggling with helping someone to set meaningful goals for themselves, we can slip back unthinkingly into an 'expert' professional stance.

There are two types of goals and it is important to think with the person about how they typically construct goals. Often when people have been distressed for some time, they understandably construe the future as getting 'away from' distressing situations or emotions. This can be helpful initially – getting away from this distress can be a powerful motivator. But over time, it helps to think about goals that they want to move 'towards'.

With 'away from' goals, the motivation to keep making progress wanes as the distance from the negative situation increases. And the reward for achieving the goal is, at best, relief. With 'towards' goals, the motivation remains high until it's achieved and the reward is a range of positive, reinforcing experiences. Table 1.1 shows how the same thing may be captured differently as an 'away from' vs 'towards' goal.

Table 1.1   'Away From' and 'Towards' goals

'Away From' goal	'Towards' goal
'To stop staying in bed all morning'	'To get out of bed and downstairs by 10am each day drinking a cup of my favourite tea'
'To stop being so critical of myself and others'	'To make one positive comment about myself and my partner each day'
'To not be in so much pain all of the time'	'To book an appointment with my GP and discuss what options I have to manage my pain so that I can spend part of each day doing something I enjoy'
'To not be so unfit'	'To do 10 minutes of something active 3 times a week'
'To not spend so much time some where I don't want to be (with family/work/other commitments)'	'To spend one hour twice a week either with people I like or doing something I enjoy'

Working out what's realistic

There are a number of elements to working out what 'realistic' means:

- where the person currently is in relation to the goals;
- where they are trying to get to and their confidence in getting there;
- why it matters to them.

Is it a goal they're really bothered about or one they feel they 'ought' to aim for? If their confidence in achieving the goal is lower than 5/10, it's important to slow down and work out what could make it more achievable. Does the goal need to be made smaller, could someone else help, does it need breaking down into smaller steps?

When you're thinking together about what they would like to achieve it really helps to bring the goal to life. Spend time thinking about what it will be like to achieve it and bringing to mind times when they have achieved similar goals before.

| IN THE SESSION ... |

An important question to spend some time thinking about and perhaps discussing with family or friends is:

- 'Where would they like to be at the end of the Steps to Recovery sessions, – what would be their realistic goals for change?'

Remind the person that they can review their goals as they progress and add more in later, so it's important to keep the goals small and focused.

The value of an 'outsider witness' in supporting recovery – identifying who will join session 8

One of the fundamental principles in the groups and individual work we have done is the importance of thinking about the people who can both support and witness the progress that the person has made on their recovery journey. Inviting people who are important in the person's life, to hear the new story, serves two functions:

- It enriches the new story through multiple retellings of the story.
- It enables a link to be made between what happens in the sessions and the rest of a person's life (Carey & Russell, 2003).

You may also have your own anxieties about this part of the process. Imagine who you would be comfortable sharing your own journey with. Going through this gives you much more compassion about how hard it can be to 'invite someone in'. And it can show you what a source of strength and support it can be when done well. If you are lucky enough to have someone you are *very* comfortable with, try sharing your ladder with someone else and note how different that feels.

This has been an interesting element for us to work through. Some people have taken to it easily, thinking quickly of someone that they would like to have support them and to come to the final session to talk about the changes they have seen the person make. For others, this part of the work has been challenging. Identifying someone that you trust enough to share your hopes with can be an intensely vulnerable experience, even just to think about. But it can also be a rich and rewarding experience for both people. Thinking through the relationships that the person has, has lost, hopes for, misses, or assumes other people have, can be very rewarding. Don't rush this bit or see it as an administrative identification of an 'appropriate person' who will be free to join you at the end of the work.

IN THE SESSION ...

This 'witness' will be invited along to the final session to talk with and about the person and the journey they have observed. So there are some key things to discuss to keep this process safe:

- How much trust do they have in this person?
- How will they talk to them about the work you are doing together?
- What is the other person's understanding of psychological distress? Is this likely to support the philosophy of recovery and the values that they will be exploring with you or is it likely to undermine it?
- Will they be free and able to come to the session? If they can't but they are the 'right' person, how else could they contribute in a way that would be meaningful?

Importantly, it is the person's responsibility to invite their 'witness' to the final session. It isn't yours to rescue or 'help'. Having that conversation is an important part of the process of building up a resilient network. Make sure that they have identified someone and have a plan for how they will be invited to the final session.

Building a bridge between this session and the next

IN THE SESSION ...

The next session will start to look at identity so, for next week, ask the person to bring something with them that is important to them or represents something of who they are. It can be anything but usually has some emotion attached to it. Ask them to think about things that they enjoy holding as well as seeing as the two senses can trigger quite different memories.

We have had photos, books, letters, cards, clothing, pebbles, poems, ticket stubs, ornaments, candles, cooking utensils, music ... brought along to our sessions.

Adding to the ladder

IN THE SESSION ...

Always try to close the session with a quick recap of what was and was not helpful and ensure that the bits they liked are in the ladder. You've covered a lot in this session so take time to pause and gather up the things that resonated with the person.

James' Story

James had been in contact with other staff in our service for a number of months before we started this specific work together and I had heard the key points when we had discussed whether the Steps to Recovery framework might help. But it was important to allow time to hear some of his story again before we went into the exercises and we took time to pull the key elements out. In that retelling was also the detail about those things that we needed to note for future sessions – what he was frightened of in the future, what he was haunted by, and what other people disagreed about (this indicated potential ruptures in his social network and expectations of what would be possible). His fears of their potential reaction helped us notice what he needed in his ladder. It also gave us space to think about who would realistically want to support him (many people) but, importantly, who he would genuinely call on in a time of trouble. I think if I'd waited until a later session or asked him directly who he could turn to, he would have cited his daughters because he felt he ought to.

The conversation about recovery took a long time and we only completed half the session. But it was invaluable. His face was so expressive and I reflected what I saw when he came alive: talking about his charity work; talking about time with his friends; talking about times when he and his wife mattered to people who had not known them long but had held them in mind and regularly got in touch.

And I noticed and talked with him about when he sagged and aged and looked lost which was often when he was talking about his family trying to protect him. This led to a conversation about his identity as a 'grown man' and balancing finding ways that his children could protect him but be enabled to let him go enough to live his life as he wanted.

This in turn led to a specific initial goal about seeing one daughter regularly and predictably (as he had before he was admitted), so that she could begin to trust his recovery and give him some space.

For James, the elements of the quote that really mattered to him were around this being personal to him – that meant it wasn't what I, his family, or the psychiatrist wanted, but what would make his life hold meaning for him. The quote gave him permission to talk about that without feeling guilty. The bit that really hooked him was the word 'contributing' – out spilled all the ways in which his previous hobbies had given him a connection with people who cared about him and the way they contributed to each other's lives. How he used those hobbies to help make other people's lives that bit easier or to raise money and how that in turn made him feel valued and that life had meaning. It would have been very easy to see his hobbies as a way of being busy and to miss the vital importance of them needing to play a specific role to be of any importance to him; whether that was being on the road here and abroad with other car enthusiasts or developing his own crafting club locally.

Mapping out his recovery journey to date really helped him see the progress he'd made. He liked using percentages and we tracked that he'd gone from near 0% to 35%, to 40% on discharge, and back to 35% at the current point. His daughters were seeing glimmers of 60% and his fear was that they were being over hopeful. At this point we talked about that being okay – they had seen a snapshot of 60% and he might have been there for 5 minutes. But it was also okay if he didn't feel like that often, if at all. Then there was a small flash of a grin talking about wanting to be 100% followed by a rapid change to assuming that wouldn't happen so 'could we talk about 75% instead'. Going back to that seemed to give him permission to just talk about what he would qualitatively see in a 75% future rather than feeling he had to be aiming for 100% in order to be taken seriously. This in turn helped us talk about the ups and downs of recovery – we drew a big set of lines about what recovery could be like similar to the graph in Figure 1.2 and we referred to it throughout our time together.

Worksheet 1.1   The Recovery Ladder

Recovery Ladder

The unique aspects that ' make up who I am:	Witnesses to my recovery:	These people are important to my recovery:
	When things wobble I can:	Barriers – things that can get in the way:
	The changes I've already made:	
	The skills I have and things I can draw on:	I can do the following to maintain these relationships:
	These things give me hope that I can recover:	

These things can make me feel worse/how I can deal with them:

Session 2

Who am I? Connecting with Identity

Drawing on the principles from Narrative Therapy this session looks at how we can help people to separate their identity from the mental health problem. The session provides conversation tips on how to strengthen a person's sense of self-identity, before looking at how to name the problem in a helpful way that empowers change.

For this session you will need

- Worksheet 2.1 The Person and the Problem
- Worksheet 2.2 Separating the Person from the Problem

Visit https://resources.sagepub.com/stepstorecovery to download

Other resources for you to refer to:

- Figure 2.2 What would someone who is close to me, say about me?
- Table 2.1 How an object might inform a person's recovery

The person not the problem

This session focuses on helping the person connect with 'who they are', despite the problem that they are experiencing. Sometimes problems can feel as though they are taking over a person's life. Telling stories about the problem over and over again (to others or in their own mind) can make it feel a VERY big part of the person's life. So much so that people often start to see the problem as part of them, part of their identity e.g. 'I am a depressive person', 'I'm an anxious person'. When the problem starts to feel part of the person, it can be very difficult to know where to start when trying to move forward in recovery.

IN THE SESSION ...

When introducing this session use Figure/Worksheet 2.1. The image aims to show that you will be trying to help the person 'pull the circles apart', i.e. separating the person from the problem.

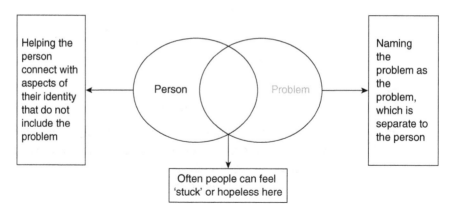

Figure 2.1 The Person and the Problem

The key message to begin the session with is around helping the person see:

'The problem is the problem ... not you! You are a unique individual and in this session the aim is to learn more about you.'

Their object and identity

At the end of the last session you will have asked the person to bring along (or keep out if working with the person at home) an object that says something about them.

IN THE SESSION ...

Ask the person to show you this object and encourage them to describe it and tell you why they chose it and why it is important.

- Encourage the person to share any stories or memories that they may have related to the object.
- What does it say about them?

Key tips and things to consider for this exercise:

Don't worry if the person has forgotten to bring an object – why not ask them to draw it or describe it without naming it and you can try to guess what it is.

- What does the object tell you about what is important to the person?
- What does the object say about the person's interests?
- What does the object suggest about the values this person tries to live by?
- Describing the object is a really important step. You will potentially get to some unexpected conversations about what is important to the person, about who they are by the way they speak about the object and the characteristics of it which they choose to prioritise. Language really matters!

Once the person has described the object and why it is important to them, start to consider if any of this learning can be used to support the person's recovery. There really is no right or wrong way of using this information to inform the recovery journey and it should be unique to the person.

It can however be tricky to consider how the description of the object and its meaning would inform recovery, so with this in mind, Table 2.1 shows a few examples from people that we have worked with.

Table 2.1 How an object might inform a person's recovery

Object	Meaning	How it informed the person's recovery
Family photograph	'My family are very important to me, especially my Grandson'	Munir described how 'the dark depression' would often 'pull me away from others, especially my family'. In talking about the family photograph, Munir identified with how spending time with his family and not talking about 'the dark depression', sometimes brought a very slight lift in his mood. He particularly enjoyed going to see his grandson play football on a Sunday, but had not been for a couple of months. Munir decided that he would try to go and watch his grandson play, but start with just watching 'the first half'. He recognised that this could connect him with his family and slightly lift his mood, which may aid his recovery.

(Continued)

Table 2.1   (Continued)

Object	Meaning	How it informed the person's recovery
Music CD (Song)	'Listening to this song takes me back to when I first met my wife. It was popular around the time we met and we even had it playing at our wedding reception'	Sam talked about how he had always enjoyed listening to music, but since 'the fear' (anxiety) had taken control of his life, he rarely had the interest or concentration to play music. During this session Sam played his favourite song and we spoke briefly about what memories it brought back. We noticed how it seemed to bring pleasure to Sam and thought about ways that he may be able to use music to help in his recovery. Sam decided to put music on some mornings when he was making breakfast, as this was often a difficult time. Rather than forcing himself to 'focus' on the music, he decided to just allow it to be in the background, which seemed to be helpful.
Pebble from a beach	'I picked up this stone from a beach where I used to walk my dog'	Lucy described the beach she used to enjoy walking along with her dog 'Peggy', before her 'dark cloud' got in the way of these walks. Lucy had not been walking her dog much since the 'dark cloud' had been around more often. We took time to mentally picture the beach and Lucy was able to describe the things she liked most about walking there ('it's not too busy and always feels calm'). Lucy felt that if she could gain the confidence to go back to walking on the beach it may help lift her mood and form part of her recovery. We then considered if there was anyone Lucy may like to take with her to the beach for support. She decided to ask her support worker to join her on the first visit for a 'short walk' with Peggy the dog. Peggy seemed pretty happy about this too!
Training shoe	'Being active has always been a big part of my life'	Joe talked about how, from being young, he was always active and enjoyed playing sport. Since the loss of his partner, Joe described how 'the black pit [depression] stopped me from feeling motivated to do anything, never mind something active'. As he was getting less physically able, he also found that the 'black pit' seemed to make him doubt his ability to do activities. We took time to consider what it was that Joe enjoyed from activities and found that it was often the sense of achievement that came at the end of completing the activity. We agreed that as part of his recovery, he would go for a very short swim at the local swimming baths. He set an achievable target of two lengths for his trip to the baths.

JR's Story

At the start of the session JR placed four photographs on the table and stated, 'these are all part of me'. There were two photographs of JR's children, a picture of JR and their partner on holiday with their sons (laughing and having fun) and a picture of JR at their former place of work. The conversations that emerged from this exercise were very powerful, emotional and important in helping JR describe who they are as a person. JR shared heart-warming stories of how they and their partner lived their life trying to bring happiness each day to both their children. Within this conversation JR remarked 'I would always say to my boys, the sun is shining, where are we going today?' which seemed to capture a philosophy of trying to take each day as it comes. Over time JR described how 'the boys would then start to say it back to me, and that was how we lived our life, one day at a time'. We agreed to add this to JR's recovery ladder as trying to take each day as it comes could also be helpful for their recovery.

How would someone who is important to you describe you?

When people are experiencing changes in their mental health it can often lower their self-esteem. This can make it very hard for people to see and connect with the positive aspects of who they are, which often leads them to see themselves in terms of the problem. Even at these difficult times people can usually, with a little encouragement, give one or two examples of how someone close to them may describe them.

IN THE SESSION ...

Ask the person to think of someone close to them. Remember that this can be absolutely anyone (pets included, as long as the person can be imaginative in what the pet 'would' say about them).

- Now ask what this person would say about them.
- Use Figure 2.2 to help.

IN THE SESSION ...

To bring this exercise to an end, discuss with the person if these aspects of their identity could in any way be helpful to help them in their recovery.

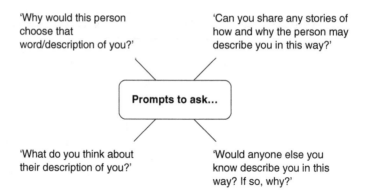

Figure 2.2   What would someone who is close to me, say about me?

We have often found that people will say something like '*well they probably used to see me as ... (organised etc.)*'. Gently remind the person that this is still part of them, even if it is tricky to connect with at the moment, with the problem getting in the way.

Examples of words and how they have been used to support the recovery of people we know include:

'*Kind*' – perhaps they could consider ways of being kind or compassionate to themselves.

'*Stubborn*' – (usually said with a raise of the eyebrows) – could this also represent determination that they can use to focus on recovery goals?

'*Family orientated*' – will it be important for the person to include their family as part of their recovery? This can also link to the final session on Outsider Witness.

'*Organised*' – might it be important for the person to use this skill when organising aspects of their day as part of their recovery?

'*Hard working*' – what was it that enabled the person to work hard? Would it be helpful for the person to share stories of when they worked hard to remind themselves that they are capable of committing to and achieving goals that they set?

Naming the problem

Now that you have started to help the person connect with aspects of their identity, it is important to help the person name the problem as something that can be thought of as separate from them. Within Narrative Therapy, this process is referred to 'Externalising' the problem (White & Epson, 1990). Sometimes simply adding a descriptive word before the problem can be a good start e.g. 'misty depression'. Adding 'the' before the problem is also a useful way to demonstrate this to the person e.g. 'what would "the" depression look like?' 'How would "the" depression like you to spend your time?'

The aim of the next activity is to help the person describe their problem in a way that allows them to identify it as separate to them. When we think about a problem as a 'thing' it can sometimes help the person feel more empowered to take a stand, or state their position in relation to the problem. Some people find this concept difficult, so it can be helpful to give lots of examples and get creative!

IN THE SESSION ...

Hand the person a blank piece of paper and ask them to:

- 'Draw me a picture of what the problem would look like if we could see it.'

If the person is struggling with how they would be able to draw the problem, offer them some prompt questions such as: What shape would it be? What colour would it be? Would it look like a person or an object? What texture would it be? How big would it be?

Or

IN THE SESSION ...

Hand the person a blank piece of paper and ask them to:

- 'Write down a few words of how you would describe the problem.'

Note of caution

There are certain things that we would not recommend naming as external to the person e.g. if they have experienced abuse of any kind. It would be invalidating to state that this is something separate to them, as it has 'happened to' the person. Think carefully about the 'problems' that have arisen which might be helpful to view from more of a distance.

Again, if the person is finding it hard to think of descriptions of the problem offer the following prompts: What personality would the problem have? Would it be sneaky or controlling? What would the problem want you to do? Is the problem considerate?

Bringing it back together (apart)

Building on the exercise you looked at in Worksheet 2.1 at the start of the session, it's important to now bring the various discussions together.

IN THE SESSION ...

Using Figure 2.3/Worksheet 2.2 Separating the person from the problem *invite the person to write/draw:*

- some key parts of their identity that they have discussed in the session in the circle on the left,
- followed by the problem in the circle on the right.
- Remember to highlight to the person that the gap between these two circles that they have been able to create allows scope for recovery to progress.

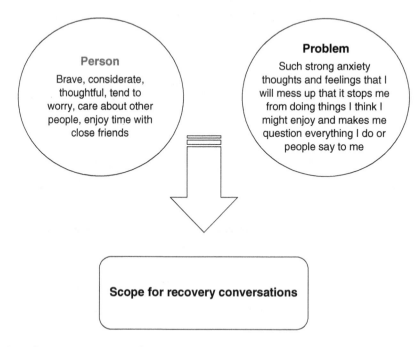

Person

Brave, considerate, thoughtful, tend to worry, care about other people, enjoy time with close friends

Problem

Such strong anxiety thoughts and feelings that I will mess up that it stops me from doing things I think I might enjoy and makes me question everything I do or people say to me

Scope for recovery conversations

Figure 2.3   Separating the person from the problem – an example

Keep it going

Now that the person has been able to separate aspects of their identity from the problem, it is important that you try to keep this distance between the two in future sessions. Perhaps the best way to do this is to keep using the language that the person has used to describe both the problem and their identity. If the person slips back into clinical descriptions of the problem e.g. depression, psychosis, anxiety, PTSD etc., try to start the next sentence with the language they had used in this session to describe the problem. It is also very important to keep coming back to their identity descriptions and consider if these characteristics/values can be helpful to draw on.

Margaret's Story

In session 5, Margaret was feeling nervous that she would not be able to complete her 'doing something different task' before the next session. Drawing on the language that had been identified in this session (2) with Margaret, the therapist asked 'What would the wobble [anxiety] want you to do?' Margaret quickly replied that the 'wobble' would want her to avoid trying to go to the hairdressers. The therapist asked in a playful manner if Margaret's 'stubborn nature' was going to let the 'wobble' get away with telling her what to do. This allowed a conversation to unfold where Margaret decided that she would try to stick to her plan despite the 'wobble' telling her she couldn't do it.

Don't take our word for it!

The 'wobble' gained its name for the problem as every time it popped up during the day or night, it would make Margaret feel unsteady. In her words it would bring about a 'wobble'.

Adding to the ladder

IN THE SESSION ...

To end the session, ask the person to make a note of the important aspects of their identity (including values and characteristics) that have been discussed in the session today.

Try to capture the language used by the person rather than your interpretation. Take time to reinforce with the person how these aspects of their identity may help support them in their recovery journey.

James' Story

James initially found this session more difficult. He really struggled to sit comfortably with talking about who he was and it took us some time to get beyond superficial descriptions. It was the objects that opened up this conversation and proved pivotal to a number of pieces of work in subsequent sessions.

He brought in a photograph of his wife and a soft toy that had accompanied them on their fundraising trips. This triggered off such a wealth of conversations about the role of those trips, the friends they'd met, the sense of purpose he'd got from them, his pride in what they had raised, his drive to help others and his fear about doing those trips alone and the responsibility that he felt for not doing any this year.

It was also a really tactile toy and it brought into the conversation the role of physical contact, loneliness and how huggable it was. We did a spider diagram of all the things the toy represented: comfort, purpose, fun, being a husband, giving back to other people, getting out and about, friends, and meeting new people.

Then we were off. We talked about people that mattered to him and the conflict around one relationship in particular (friend 1). We drew out some charts showing those relationships and he shaded in how strong he thought those relationships were. That enabled us to look at where the main gaps were between where things were and where he wanted them to be. It also allowed him to say that some would never be 100% safe/okay because his wife wouldn't be with him and that was alright – he didn't want to aim for a false 100%. He was happy with some of those staying at a meaningful 50%. He was also then able to prioritise them and focus on one at a time, knowing that we would come back to the others later. He brought this to every session.

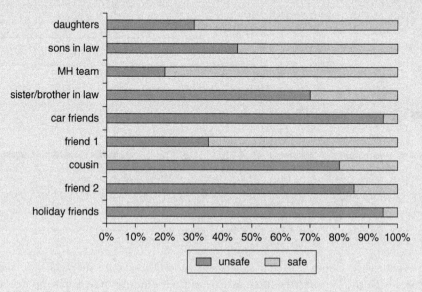

Figure 2.4   Feeling unsafe and safe with relationships: Session 2

And then we moved on to what he did with his time. This changed a lot over the sessions as he came to decide that he could allow himself to stop trying to replicate the life he'd had with his wife (the hole that was left by her not being there was too large) and that he could start to build a new chapter of his life. The metaphor with stories and chapters was perfect for James. Moving to a new chapter didn't un-write what had gone before; the book was still being written.

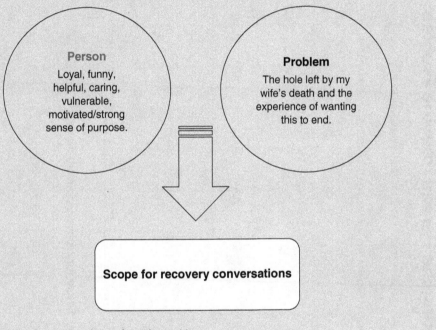

Person

Loyal, funny, helpful, caring, vulnerable, motivated/strong sense of purpose.

Problem

The hole left by my wife's death and the experience of wanting this to end.

Scope for recovery conversations

Figure 2.5   Separating James from the problem

Worksheet 2.2   Separating the Person from the Problem

1. In the circle to the left marked 'person', make a list of all the elements of the person's identity that you have learnt in the session today.
2. Next in the circle to the right, write or draw the descriptor of the problem that the person has identified.
3. Finally discuss the importance of keeping this space between the two as part of recovery conversations.

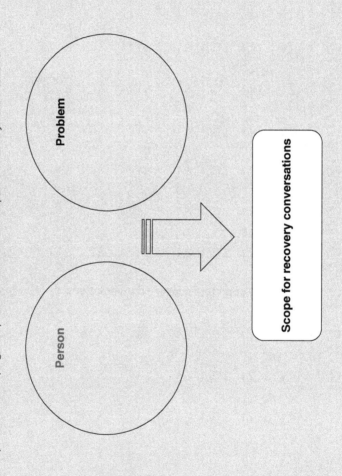

Person

Problem

Scope for recovery conversations

Session 3

Understanding Mental Health: Perceptions, Stigma and Myths

This session focuses on understanding, from a broad perspective, what is meant by mental wellbeing or distress, the cultural ideas that surround the way it is perceived and working together to understand the specific things that might affect the mental health of the person you are working with.

For this session you will need:

- Worksheet 3.1 Myth or Fact? (question and answer sheets)
- NB you will also need to be prepared, either with access to the internet or magazines, to look for famous people that the person you are working with is interested in and see whether they have any history of problems with their mental health. This is worth putting some preparation time into.

(Continued)

(Continued)

Visit https://resources.sagepub.com/stepstorecovery to download

Other resources for you to refer to:

- Table 3.1 General examples of things that can negatively affect our mental wellbeing

Wellbeing and the environment: it matters where you are able to spend your time

The session is structured first around general exercises to help you think together about the person's understanding of mental health in general, before thinking about factors that are more relevant to them personally. We have always understood mental wellbeing as something that is strongly influenced by the social context in which a person lives. If, for example, someone feels valued within their community, has access to things that matter to them, and is able to live with the freedom of personal and family safety, then they are much more likely to experience a sense of psychological wellbeing than someone who doesn't. Similarly, recovering from a period of distress is inevitably affected by the social environment in which the person has grown up, now lives, and imagines for their (possible) future/s.

Conversations about social messages that the person has internalised or deliberately rejected (or indeed remains unsure about) are important if they are going to build a framework that stands a chance of lasting. The various exercises in this session encourage you to take a variety of perspectives and introduce the potential for creating a new and more helpful narrative that sets up a recovery orientated future.

Stigma and society

As we discussed in session 2, strengthening the idea that a person's identity is separate from the 'problem' (whatever words they and others use to describe it) can empower change. However, this can be made all the more challenging when 'the problem' forms part of a much wider cultural narrative of mental health, which may be deeply internalised. Within our work, we encounter on an almost daily basis the wide range of cultural narratives, both positive and stigmatising, that are attached to concepts of mental health. Interestingly, people will often say that they don't believe the stigma, but it is incredibly difficult not to absorb it at some level. Stigmatising narratives can be seductive and appear on the surface to hold some truth and are therefore often difficult to challenge.

The hearers of the story believed that it was true because it was meaningful, rather than it was meaningful because it was true. (Doan & Alan, 1994: 2)

Individuals are also more likely to be caught up in narratives about mental health that are, or have been, dominant in their own culture and this can vary widely. It's important therefore to think further about cultural perceptions of mental health and the way that this affects how true these feel to the person you are working with. We've labelled this Myths and Facts but in some ways that plays into the idea that there are 'truths' about mental health and distress. There are correlations and theories but, as a quick look at social and traditional media or academic articles will show, we are a long way off from an agreed understanding of what causes distress or, conversely, enables people to cope.

IN THE SESSION ...

To open up conversation on this area, consider asking the following questions:

- How do you think the society you live in views mental health? This might be nationally or a much more local community.
- Think about the way people talk about it and what is said (and not said) in the media. What images are used?

Everybody has mental health problems at some point in their lives, even if the severity and extent of it differ.

IN THE SESSION ...

Myth or Fact? Look through Worksheet 3.1 and talk with the person about the various statements.

- At its simplest you can look at which are 'true' or 'false' but the conversation is often much richer if you can also think about the impact of those beliefs on them and other people.
- How do those beliefs affect the person's expectations of themselves, their recovery and the role that other people might play in the future?

Use the conversation to think about how the community in which the person lives views struggles with mental wellbeing. Listen to the language that they use. Where are they hearing that language? Is it in social media, the news, films, books, conversations with friends? And what is not said? What messages do they not hear about mental wellbeing and distress? What does that imply is 'possible', 'expected' or 'ruled out'?

Instead of just going through the lists of myths/facts, write them out separately on cards and, between you, choose a few that you are most interested in. A really engaged conversation about three of them is better than 'churning' through them all like a test!

Challenging the myths about psychological distress can be a good way to get people thinking and talking about mental health and the beliefs that they and others hold about their experiences.

It can also be helpful to think about whether other people that are important to them would have a very different response to any of the statements – that can help to highlight any relationships where they might feel less secure or have concerns about the reaction to their current situation.

In the worksheet we have given our answers to whether we think that the statements are true or not. But this is the least important part of the discussion. You or they might have a very different view to us and that's okay. The real value of this discussion is in them thinking about whether any of those myths or facts matter to them and those around them. Even if the person themselves doesn't agree with the 'myths' do they think you do? Or their family? Would that change what the person feels it is 'acceptable' to hope for? Or how they talk about their experiences? Does it make it more/less likely that they would ask for help if they felt unwell?

IN THE SESSION ...

Has that conversation highlighted anything that it would be useful to add to their ladder? For example things that might make them feel worse, or give them hope, or the people who are important to them.

Who experiences mental health problems?

Some people get a lot from this exercise and other people don't find it adds value. As with all the exercises discuss it together and decide together how to best use it.

IN THE SESSION ...

Search online or in magazines for some famous people that the person likes.

- Try to identify whether or not that individual is known to have experienced mental health difficulties. (Note – it can be helpful for you to already have some famous people in mind to search for who are known to have experienced mental health difficulties e.g. Ruby Wax, Stephen Fry, Lemn Sissay).

- Does the discussion create any surprises?
- How does that affect what they choose to put on their ladder? Perhaps in terms of their skills, hopes or things they can do when they 'wobble' in their recovery.

Factors affecting mental health

There is an endless list of things that may affect a person's mental health and sense of wellbeing (see Table 3.1). However, it is not very often that people get the chance to pause and reflect on these factors in detail; that is the purpose of the following exercise.

This is a much more powerful exercise if the person themselves goes and seeks out information about people either from their own culture or people that they respect who have talked about their own mental health problems. It's better to identify one person who they are surprised or inspired by than have a long list of 'meaningless' celebrities that they don't care about either way.

IN THE SESSION ...

Ask the person what kind of things they think can have an impact *(for better or worse)* on their mental health?

- If they struggle with this start to look for patterns together.
- This might be an exercise that they look into over the next few weeks and ask other people for help with.

This is not what *you* think affects their mental health or what their family thinks but what *they* think. You might ask if you can offer any observations from things you've heard but only if it feels appropriate. It might also be powerful to ask whether other people would make the same list for themselves (this might give some additional ideas for the person's own list) or for the person you are working with (which might lead to some interesting conversations about the different ways people conceptualise their mental wellbeing).

We have found this to be a golden opportunity to normalise a conversation about mental wellbeing by sharing the factors that affect our own mental health. People are often surprised to hear that there are many common factors that impact on most people's wellbeing such as: poor sleep, family relationships, transitions, loss, feeling out of control, feeling unable to find an answer to a problem, feeling unable to meet demands placed on you, poor health, the weather, the news, feeling powerless.

Authors' thoughts – what affects our mental health?

Sarah: Apart from the obvious ones (people I care about being well and feeling I can cope with challenges e.g. financial or work demands) ... being stagnant, no change happening or problems not being in the process of being solved, people saying one thing and doing another. Not spending time with people who I find interesting. Not getting outside every day. Poor sleep and not enough fresh food. Too much caffeine.

Graeme: Not getting the chance to exercise regularly can have all kinds of negative impact on my mental health, but most noticeably it leads me to feel 'sluggish' and tired during the day. Working too late at night and not leaving enough time to 'wind down' can affect my sleep, which in turn affects my sense of wellbeing. Taking on too many demands without enough time can also be unhelpful and leave me feeling unable to relax.

Table 3.1   General examples of things that can negatively affect mental wellbeing

The physical environment where we live	Isolation	Having to depend on other people for help
Someone else in the family experiencing mental health problems	Thinking about/ being reminded about past events	Social or cultural expectations that don't fit with what we want to do
Loss	Life changes	How and where we can relax
Having an argument with a family member or friend	Physical disability	Putting too much pressure on ourselves
Whether we have close family and friends	Ill health / Infections	Retirement
Place of work	Not seeing other people for periods of time	Using alcohol or drugs
Not eating very well	Not taking prescribed medications	Some genetic conditions (heredity)
Not being able to leave the house	Spending a lot of time thinking about something that causes me concern	Not getting enough sleep

> ### IN THE SESSION ...
>
> As you go through this exercise, encourage the person to add to their ladder so that they don't lose thoughts that they've had. They can always amend the ladder at any point if they change their mind.

Self-care

We encourage you to take some time to think with the person about how they look after their wellbeing on a regular basis rather than just creating a plan for when things start to go wrong. A lot of people get a skewed idea that self-care is a lavish, one-off event that we do when we remember or feel inclined to. We think that's an unhelpful way to approach it. One obstacle in that approach is that when you feel low it can be hard to either motivate yourself to do those 'lavish' things or to believe that you're worth the effort. The trick is not to make it demanding or unusual. Self-care is a habit built up of lots of small decisions and behaviours and the more habitual something becomes the less demanding it is. If the person doesn't feel that they are 'worth' the self-care now, it can help to think about their future self and externalise the process somewhat. What small daily things can they do that their future self would appreciate? This will vary widely but here are some of the ways we take care of our future selves:

- Buying some fresh food at the weekend and making a few lunches up for the week.
- Going to bed 20 minutes earlier.
- Ironing an outfit for work the night before.
- Filling up with fuel on the way home rather than leaving it to the morning rush.
- Choosing not to spend time with people who don't like me.
- Regularly doing some small things that make me nervous so I keep the practice in and they don't overwhelm me later.

JR's Story

JR arrived for session 3 looking a little more tired than usual. When this was reflected back to them, JR commented that they were currently having their bathroom refurbished and that 'the stress of it all', was taking its toll on JR's mental health. JR made an interesting observation that things such as home improvement would never have typically affected their mental health in the past, but since leaving work they have more time to 'worry' about disruptions such as this. JR noted that 'different things affect people at different times in their life' and it is important to think about how this may change. After some discussion on the matter, JR decided to write on their recovery ladder that 'change', 'unpredictability' and 'too much time to think' can all affect their mental health.

Adding to the ladder

Ask the person if there is anything that could be helpfully added to their ladder e.g.:

- 'When things wobble I can ...'
- 'The skills I have and things I can draw on are ...'
- 'These are the small regular things I can do to take care of myself'
- or 'These things can make me feel worse/how I can deal with them'.

James' Story

For James this was difficult in that it opened up lots of 'shameful' (to him) thoughts about how he used to perceive mental health problems. He struggled to reconcile this with his new understanding of how many people actually experience this level of distress and how he had felt over the last two years.

We matched up a couple of types of statement; those that indicated people might experience stigma and the high prevalence rates. Mapping these onto his experiences led us to a number of very helpful conversations. The most important was the core role of his family and friends in his recovery. From there we thought about his statements that 'they will be fine, I'm not worried about them' but his fear was in fact that they might not be. From that we began to set, as a priority, goals around meeting them all at least three times because that seemed to be the 'magic' number of times that he needed before he could trust that things were 'okay' between him and them.

We kept notes about his fears of what would happen. He was concerned that relatives would hold the same beliefs that he had previously held and therefore worried about 'what will they think of me and what I've done'. But his actual experience was that no one was any different with him, other than that his immediate family were worried about him.

As we talked about the elements of his identity that he really cared about, we began to think about goals related to his need to make his own decisions. Balancing his goal for self-determination with wanting to protect and maintain relationships with his relatives, we then built in a sub-goal about giving them enough information about his plans so that they could relax whilst also giving him the space he needed.

Worksheet 3.1   Myth or Fact?

Challenging the myths about mental illness can be a good way to think and talk about mental health. In this exercise, read each of the statements and decide whether or not you believe that the statement is a myth or fact.

	Myth or Fact?
People diagnosed with mental illness can't work.	
Mental health problems are very rare.	
People with mental illness never recover.	
People with mental health problems are different from normal people.	
After experiencing a mental health problem, people are weaker.	
People diagnosed with mental illnesses are violent and unpredictable.	
It's best to leave people alone if they develop a mental health problem.	
I don't know anyone with a mental illness.	
People aren't discriminated against because of mental health problems.	
People with mental health problems are different from normal people.	
After experiencing a mental health problem, people are weaker.	

Worksheet 3.1   Myth or Fact answers

Myth: People diagnosed with a mental illness can't work.

Fact: Chances are, you probably work with someone who has been diagnosed with a mental illness.

Myth: Mental health problems are very rare.

Fact: Mental health problems affect one in four people.

Myth: People with mental illness never recover.

Fact: People with mental illness can and do recover.

Myth: People with mental health problems are different from normal people.

Fact: We all have mental health problems, just like we all have physical health problems at various times in life.

Myth: After experiencing a mental health problem, people are weaker.

Fact: Many people who have gone through experiences like this actually feel stronger.

Myth: People diagnosed with mental illnesses are violent and unpredictable.

Fact: People diagnosed with mental illness are more likely to be a victim of violence.

Myth: It's best to leave people alone if they develop a mental health problem.

Fact: Most people with mental health problems want to keep in touch with friends, family and colleagues, it can be a great help in their recovery.

Myth: I don't know anyone with a mental illness.

Fact: Someone you know or love has likely experienced a mental illness.

Myth: People aren't discriminated against because of mental health problems.

Fact: Nine out of ten people with mental health problems experience stigma and discrimination.

Session 4
Hope and Recovery

This session explores ways in which you can help to foster hope for a person's recovery. Short recovery stories and 'inspirational' quotes are provided, alongside ways to reflect on times the person has recovered from difficult situations in the past.

For this session you will need

- Worksheet 4.1 Inspirational Quotes

Visit https://resources.sagepub.com/stepstorecovery to download

Having a sense of hope is key

Experiencing psychological distress can lead a person to view themselves, their world and their future in a negative way. Often people who are recovering from mental health difficulties will describe moments where they feel minimal hope or total hopelessness. When looking at the stories told by those who have recovered from mental health difficulties, research finds that having a sense of hope is key in the early phase of recovery (Young & Ensing, 1999). Trying to foster hope is therefore essential in supporting the person to experience a sense of direction and momentum for their recovery journey. If the person can believe that hope is possible, they are far more likely to feel able to have a go at some of the changes they might want to make.

IN THE SESSION ...

Start the session by explaining that having a sense of hope has been shown to be very important to give direction and momentum to a person's recovery.

- Ask the person what they think about this and allow some time for open conversation.

As an example of recovery data in a specific context – Improving Access to Psychological Therapy (NHS in England) reported in Jan 2018 that 50.7% of people receiving therapy report 'moving to recovery' following psychological therapy (Health and Social Care Information Centre, 2018).

A common question asked by many people that we work with, particularly in the early stages of their recovery is: 'Will I recover from this ...?' or 'Will I ever get better?' There is always a human dilemma in this situation. This question presents a perfect opportunity to start developing hope and it is very tempting to just blurt out 'yes of course!' in a desperate attempt to seize the moment and 'give' the person hope. The chances are, however, that they will have been 'reassured' before and the fact that they are asking means they still don't believe it. It can be superficial and patronising to rush in with 'yes' when you actually have no idea. But it can also be demoralising and soulless to ignore it or say 'I don't know'.

What can provide a sense of hope is the genuine assurance that you are prepared to work on this with them and see where it takes you. This framework is one source of ideas that you can work through together, finding what helps and ignoring what doesn't. Some people also find hope in facts and real stories of other people's recovery.

It would be helpful if there was a golden statistic to offer in this type of conversation e.g. 'well the evidence tells us that this amount of people recover from mental health difficulties ...'.

But, as you may have guessed, this doesn't meaningfully exist and with good reason. As we discussed at the start of this book, recovery is a deeply personal and subjective experience. As such it is hard to capture exact numbers about how many people feel they have reached a position in their recovery that they are happy with rather than data on observable 'symptoms'. If the person you are working with would like you to comment on a recovery figure, you can always look at the outcome data for a particular condition or diagnosis but think back to their views on illness models and diagnoses from earlier sessions before you do that.

JR's Story

The topic of having and holding on to hope arose time and time again during JR's Steps to Recovery sessions. This was in part related to the multiple physical illness challenges that they faced along the way. When discussing the importance of hope within one session JR remarked 'you feel like you just have hold of that rope (hope) and that it is starting to pull you forward, but then something comes along and it (hope) is pulled from your grasp'. We spent time acknowledging that hope can come and go, just like a sense of recovery and wellness. For JR it was important to have something concrete to hold in mind when trying to re-establish a sense of hope. JR found it helpful to vividly recall how they felt and what they were doing when they last recovered from 'the dark mist' (depression), in order to believe that it is possible again.

More than 'positive thinking'

So how is hope different to 'positive thinking'? Positive thinking is often used to describe a deliberate change in the way in which people think, 'choosing' to move away from negative thoughts and focusing on thoughts that are more future focused. However, hope is about a person's belief that they can recover from their difficulties. It is

Note of caution

Hope cannot be forced and it's not just 'positive thinking'.

about a fundamental shift in perspective, not just the thoughts that they may be experiencing in that particular moment. So, while hope may well bring with it more positive thinking, it represents a change in belief and outlook that can help motivate the person towards recovery.

Trying to help people develop a sense of hope can feel like a significant challenge, but there are a number of ways it might be fostered:

- Knowing and seeing that others believe in them.
- Listening to other people's recovery stories.
- Having a network of support which fosters hope that they will recover as they are not alone.

- A more detailed understanding about mental health increases a sense of personal control and brings with it a sense of hope.
- Celebrating small changes not only develops but also, importantly, maintains a sense of hope.

Inspiration

We have found that this is a good opportunity to share what kinds of people inspire us. We have shared many examples such as Terry Waite for his openness about his own struggles and his combination of acceptance and determination when held hostage in the 1980s.

Sometimes people find that looking to others can help to bring inspiration and hope that people can and do recover. Inspiration, like recovery, often comes in different forms and it can be helpful to start to tap into what kind of things and/or individuals may inspire the person you are working with.

Inspirational stories

IN THE SESSION ...

Ask the person whether they have ever come across someone who has appeared to overcome something that was difficult? •

- Ask the person to describe this to you and listen to how they talk about the problem, the other person and what they did.
- Was there anything about this person and what they did that they found inspirational?

Listen carefully to how they describe the person that overcame something difficult. What did they focus on and why? We often hear people referring to things such as courage, determination and compassion. The reason for this exercise is not to focus on super-human people who the rest of us cannot possibly live up to. In fact the person being described probably doesn't feel like they are superhuman either. The point of the exercise is to start to break down what other people do when they are faced with a problem and then think about what the person you are supporting already has to hand or could learn from them.

If the person can't think of someone 'real' then it's fine to use fictional characters that inspire them. One of us was coached recently thinking about how a superhero would help us in a tricky situation and now channels Batman at regular intervals at work!

IN THE SESSION ...

Do they think that some of this person's values or characteristics would be helpful for them to have with them in their recovery?

Perhaps consider with the person, how these particular values and characteristics may be helpful. When we speak about those who inspire us, we often see the traits or values that they hold as something that is out of reach or beyond us. This may be particularly true when experiencing mental health difficulties. The main aim here is to try and help the person think about how and why that *characteristic or skill* that inspires them could be useful in the recovery journey, and how it could be put into action.

Putting the *thing* that inspires the person into action can again feel a little abstract at times. How would the person just be more 'determined' or 'wise'? It's worth taking time to consider what that may look like in the person's life. For example 'determination' can be broken down from a broad descriptive term into small actions that represent 'determination to stand up to the problem' e.g. being determined to set the table for breakfast. We have also found it useful to ask the person to consider whether these characteristics would be obvious to themselves or others as part of their recovery. For example 'compassion' could be shown to the self by the person noticing and responding hopefully when the problem makes them critical of themselves, but it could also be shown to a family member by asking how they are feeling even though the person finds it hard to engage in such conversations.

Inspirational quotes

Sometimes being distressed is just really complicated and messy and, amongst all the advice you're given or frameworks you can work through, you just need one thing to easily hold on to. For some people there's nothing as helpful as a quote that resonates with them and becomes a soothing mantra. Other people get nothing from them. You'll quickly see whether this grabs the person you're working with.

IN THE SESSION ...

Looking together at Worksheet 4.1, ask the person to read through the list of quotes and see if any of them jump out at them.

- What is it about that quote that feels important?
- What could they do to help themselves remember it?
- Are there any that they really don't like – what is it helpful to take from that?

Don't take our word for it!

For Nina this quote stood out '*If all you can do is crawl, start crawling.*' Nina found this particularly helpful to look at first thing in the morning. As she put it, even crawling out of bed can be difficult when 'the depression' wants you to go back under the covers. Taking it slow and steady often came to her mind when looking at this quote.

We have found that encouraging the person to focus on one or two quotes increases the chance that they will be used regularly. It can also sometimes be helpful to encourage the person to think of ways in which they may be able to refer back to the quote. This may be particularly helpful on the more challenging days in their recovery journey. They may wish to write the quote on a piece of paper and place it on their fridge door, beside their bed, in their wallet, in a drawer they regularly use.

Learning from previous recovery

It would be unusual for someone to have got to the adult phase of life and not have had some setback that they have managed to get through. This can provide a source of important learning about existing strengths. It can be hard when things are difficult and the person feels unable to remember times when they have managed and felt more able (in fact that's how our brains work – they remember things which are similar to how we currently feel). So spending time thinking about how they have problem-solved in the past can make a significant difference.

IN THE SESSION ...

Ask the person if they can think of a time when they have got through a difficult experience in the past. e.g. *a difficult loss, ill health, a period of feeling stuck.*

They don't need to have completely resolved it or done it all themselves. Just think about a problem that they've had that eventually got even slightly better.

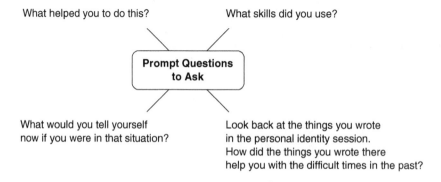

Figure 4.1 Helping the person think about how they got through previously difficult situations

JR's Story

When looking at how JR could learn from times when they had previously survived difficulty, we spoke of a deeply personal experience. JR reflected back on how devastating it was to have lost two young children to physical illness, within 18 months of each other. No words seemed able to capture the unimaginable devastation that JR and their partner went through at this time and it felt important to understand how JR 'kept going'.

JR talked of how their children would have many difficult days with their physical illness, yet they would always find the courage to keep 'living life'. JR returned to the common question their sons would ask; 'the sun is shining, where are we going today ...?' This seemed to represent the idea that no matter how difficult the situation may be, JR and their children were able to seize the little moments of sunshine to make the most of that moment. We agreed to keep a note of this in JR's recovery ladder along with the quote from the children in order to hold on to the concept of trying to focus on each moment as it comes.

Recovery is possible – for some, it can be helpful to hear other people's recovery stories, to draw hope that recovery is possible. We often find that the closer the recovery story is to the circumstances that the person is going through (e.g. loss, depression, anxiety, psychosis etc.) the more they can relate it to their recovery journey. If you have time at the end of the session, you may like to share some example stories. It's useful to have a look online for ones that may be most suitable before the session. As an example, we have found some of the recovery stories on this website useful to share with individuals: www.mentalhealth.org.uk/stories

Adding to the ladder

IN THE SESSION ...

Is there a quote, a name or a specific characteristic (of themselves or someone else) that the person would like to add to their ladder? It can be cryptic, fun or very serious. Whatever will help the person make use of it in the future.

James' Story

By this point James had consistently reached 55–60% with a low of 50% and no 'bad nights'. This was the first period of time where he had started to believe that this progress could be sustained; 'Maybe I could think about 100 per cent, it's the first time I've dared to imagine it'.

(Continued)

(Continued)

James had a completely different reaction to the crawling quote that Nina liked. He found this threatening and couldn't contemplate being that unwell. For our work together, knowing what he really wasn't comfortable with was almost more helpful than the ones he liked as, by that point, we had got to know each other fairly well. (This is a good reminder that there is no right or wrong way to engage with the material. Both James and Nina benefited from the work, just in different ways.)

James liked these quotes:

- Start by doing what's necessary; then do what's possible; and suddenly you are doing the impossible. – *St. Francis of Assisi*
- Do what you can, with what you have, where you are. – *Theodore Roosevelt*
- You are never too old to set another goal or to dream a new dream. – *C.S. Lewis*

We had a lovely conversation about his practical approach to life, his determination to solve things and to make the best of what he had. It also led to an unexpected conversation about one decision he had made that he perceived retrospectively as being about proving to others that he 'still could'.

In a really touching turn of events, James then began to talk about his own 'rules' about life and we created his own 'quote'. For those of you with training in therapy models this felt similar to elements of CBT. But tagging it as a personal quote rather than a 'rule for living' made it something that belonged to him.

'I've spent my whole life proving to myself that I can succeed and I like to see the result. I'm proving I can build a new chapter of my life'.

We've talked about listening carefully to the language the person uses. For James, I was concerned about his use of 'absolutes'. For example, we really had to think about what 'always succeed' meant as there were times when that became quite damaging – not everything that went through his head was something he really wanted to succeed at but he could then get stuck on 'not succeeding' rather than finding what mattered to him. When we thought it through, although his memory was that things had 'just gone well', there had been many small actions towards that outcome (not a clear route to success), and lots of things that didn't go so well, but had combined to create a 'successful' outcome over a longer period. From that we concluded that it was okay that some things weren't going perfectly at the moment.

Worksheet 4.1 Inspirational Quotes

- Change your thoughts and you change your world. *Norman Vincent Peale*
- When we deny the story, it defines us. When we own the story, we can write a brave new ending. *Henry David Thoreau*
- If you don't like something, change it; if you can't change it, change the way you think about it. *Mary Engelbreit*
- Until we are able to use our own words to tell our own stories, the context we find ourselves in ... says our stories for us, and usually gets it wrong ... When he proclaimed: 'You have a mental illness.' I responded: 'I thought I had a story to tell.' *Beth Filson*
- He who has health, has hope; and he who has hope, has everything. *Thomas Carlyle*
- Know what's weird? Day by day, nothing seems to change, but pretty soon ... everything's different. *Bill Watterson*
- Often the key part of the journey from chaos to clarity is telling the story. Stories give us a handle on how we feel and an ability to tolerate and accept those feelings. *Tanya Byron*
- There is nothing like returning to a place that remains unchanged to find the ways in which you yourself have altered. *Nelson Mandela*
- If all you can do is crawl, start crawling. *Rumi*
- When we cannot find a way of telling our story, our story tells us – we dream these stories, we develop symptoms, or we find ourselves acting in ways we don't understand. *Stephen Grosz*
- Never apologize for being sensitive or emotional. Let this be a sign that you've got a big heart and aren't afraid to let others see it. Showing your emotions is a sign of strength. *Brigitte Nicole*
- The journey of a thousand miles begins with a single step. *Lao Tzu*
- Whenever we talk about ourselves we tell stories. Without these stories, our experiences would sit – unconnected – like a thousand tiny beads. *Lucy Waddington*
- Do not wait until the conditions are perfect to begin. Beginning makes the conditions perfect. *Alan Cohen*
- I always managed to return to my story and thus was able to preserve my sanity and identity. *Terry Waite*
- Start by doing what's necessary; then do what's possible; and suddenly you are doing the impossible. *St. Francis of Assisi*
- You don't have to be great to start, but you have to start to be great. *Joe Sabah*
- More powerful than the will to win is the courage to begin. *Unknown*
- You can't stop the waves, but you can learn to surf. *Jon Kabat Zin*
- Our job is not to deny the story but to defy the ending. To rise strong, recognise our story; rumble with the truth until we get to a place where we think, Yes. This is what happened, this is my truth, and I will choose how this story ends. *Brené Brown*
- I do ... to this day, think that success is being able to look in the mirror and know that I'm alright on that day. I don't believe I've made it – I believe that I'm making it. *Lemn Sissay*
- From small beginnings come great things. *Proverb*
- Do what you can, with what you have, where you are. *Theodore Roosevelt*

- A hard beginning maketh a good ending. *John Heywood*
- Nobody can go back and start a new beginning, but anyone can start today and make a new ending. *Maria Robinson*
- You are never too old to set another goal or to dream a new dream. *C.S. Lewis*
- I like living. I have sometimes been wildly, despairingly, acutely miserable, racked with sorrow, but through it all I still know that just to be alive is a grand thing. *Agatha Christie*
- Fall seven times, stand up eight. *Japanese proverb*
- Our greatest weakness lies in giving up. The most certain way to succeed is always to try just one more time. *Thomas Edison*
- Dreams are renewable. No matter what our age or condition, there are still untapped possibilities within us and new beauty waiting to be born. *Helen Keller*

Session 5

Harnessing Skills and Resources: Doing Something Different

This session focuses on helping the person to identify the skills and personal resources that they possess that might assist them in their recovery. We introduce some exercises to help the person recognise the difference between skills and resources, before considering how they might both be helpful. The second part of the session introduces ways of supporting the person to 'do something different' as part of their recovery.

For this session you will need

- Worksheet 5.1 Trying Something New

Visit https://resources.sagepub.com/stepstorecovery to download

Other resources for you to refer to:

- Figure 5.1 Balancing the feedback that you give people
- Figure 5.2 Different types of resource
- Figure 5.3 General features of where people live
- Figure 5.4 One of our 'maps'
- Table 5.1 What positive risk taking is and is not

Using skills and resources to try something different

This session is split into two parts. The first part of the session builds on the identity and inspirational people exercises and looks at the skills and resources the person possesses, which might be helpful in the future. There are exercises for exploring this if it isn't obvious to the person what they do have access to. We also give examples from ourselves and people we have worked with. The second part of the session explores how 'doing something different' can be an important part of the recovery journey. It looks at the term 'positive risk taking' and what that is and is not and provides ways of thinking about what the person themselves would like to do differently.

This session covers a lot of material. Make sure that the person keeps putting ideas on their ladder as you go through so that they don't lose anything that is important to them.

Part 1: Skills and resources

Cultural narratives in physical and mental health are inherently problem focused. This is of course with good reason, as it's rare that someone goes to their GP and starts a conversation off with 'I want to tell you about how well I'm coping'. We typically go with problems in mind, looking for help and hoping that others have the skills to bring about change. It is therefore important to name this process, and to ensure people feel 'okay' to speak about their skills and resources in the session.

This session focuses on building the ladder to recovery by thinking about the many skills and resources that the person already has. We've found that this can feel like an uncomfortable session simply because many people are not used to speaking out loud about the things that they are good at. That has sometimes been because they feel embarrassed, as if it's boasting, and it's important to clearly acknowledge that this might be very different from the conversations that have surrounded their mental health in the past.

They might be used to conversations that focus on need, risk, 'problems' and diagnosis (both within and outside of services). The very reason they are seeking support might be because people around them don't often acknowledge the person's own strengths, which makes even noticing and naming them difficult. This is where it can be really helpful to think about the role that you and other people play in the process.

There is a balance to be had here (different for everyone) between:

- overwhelming the person with a positive picture of themselves that they do not recognise and is too far from their own current 'truth' to hear;
- and contributing gentle prompts to help someone look for a different view of themselves.

As Figure 5.1 demonstrates, too much and people can feel that you or others are showering them in fake praise, too little and you risk not harnessing their real skills and resources.

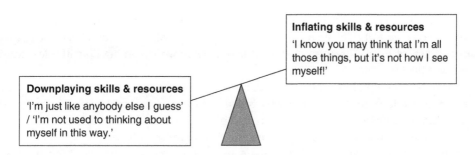

Inflating skills & resources
'I know you may think that I'm all those things, but it's not how I see myself!'

Downplaying skills & resources
'I'm just like anybody else I guess' / 'I'm not used to thinking about myself in this way.'

Figure 5.1 Balancing the feedback that you give people

We've realised how many assumptions and limitations people place on themselves when thinking about skills and resources, so here is what we mean by the terms.

- **Skills** – are internal to the person. They are the way in which they can translate their knowledge into useful (to them or to others) behaviour.
- **Resources** – are external to the person. They are the things that they can draw on for help. They may often carry positive and negative features in terms of how much they can support the person's recovery.

The person's skills

Often people approach this session as a concrete and dry conversation akin to a job interview and, as a result, the skills and resources they generate are limited and unconsciously linked to things that are valued in the culture in which they live. For us and many of the people we work with these are often Western capitalist values of hard work, money, ability to 'do' something, 'expert' knowledge and productivity. As we discussed in session 3, these pervasive messages are often some of the things that cause problems in the first place. The exercises below will help you explore their skills in a more supportive way.

IN THE SESSION ...

Invite the person to write a list of the skills they think they possess.

- Don't limit this to skills that are obviously related to mental wellbeing. The more creative and diverse they can be, the more you will have to work with.
- If the person struggles, think with them about where/when they experience a sense of being comfortable and at ease or wanted and valued – what skills do they draw on in those situations?
- Once they have a list of skills you can then begin to think together about where these skills might be useful.

For example, playing netball might not seem immediately related to recovery but probably covers a whole host of skills such as commitment, fitness, making friends, being able to maintain routines, planning, organising, quick thinking, team work, coming up with ideas for the team, and the list could go on.

One of the unhelpful ironies of life is that the things we are good at tend to be the things that we notice least in ourselves exactly because they are so second nature to us. It's the things that we struggle with that we notice and overestimate in other people. We're all aware of our own internal struggles, it's everyone else that seems so polished.

If the person is struggling with this there are various strategies you can both try. If you start from the premise that skills are knowledge or values that translate into behaviour, you can start the conversation with the values that matter to them.

IN THE SESSION ...

Talk together about what the person thinks it is important to do/be in order to be the person they want to be? ... *Kind, generous, thoughtful, strong, decisive, quiet, calm, passionate, protective ...?*

What do they do (remembering that none of us are 100% anything) that reflects those values? ... *Remembers people's birthdays, stands up for other people, keeps the peace, makes decisions and acts on them ...*

IN THE SESSION ...

Once you have the list go back through and think about the skills that they are inclined to dismiss and use the prompts below to help think through why that might be.

It can be helpful to think about what other people would say. Encourage the person to write those skills down for now even if they don't agree with them.

- If it's not true, why would someone else say it?
  - o Often we get back 'because they're nice and would want to make me feel better'.
  - o So what is it about the person you're working with that would make someone else want to do that for them? Is it, for example, that they are kind, helpful, thoughtful?
  - o Could those words go on the list instead?

- Is the person thinking that they have to feel 100% confident in those skills or demonstrate them consistently for them to 'count'?

    o   None of us exhibits any characteristic or skill all the time and skills that we might find easy to use in one part of our life can feel near impossible in another. If they've ever demonstrated those skills in any part of life, put them on the list. They are still skills they have even if they need a bit of support to strengthen them and use them more often.

- Could they take some time before your next session to ask the friend/relative what they meant when they used that word about them? Or could they spend some time more carefully watching how people talk about them and to them and what that suggests they think about the skills the person has?

There are times when we have asked whether we can offer our own thoughts on the skills that we have seen the person display in the time we have known them. Our own learning is to use this carefully and sparingly, but that it can be very powerful.

IN THE SESSION ...

Offer one or two words with some evidence to back it up and then let the person think about this and decide whether it fits well enough with them.

A couple of words is much better than overwhelming them with a long list of gushing attributes that you struggle to back up or which leave the person feeling railroaded and unable to disagree with you.

For situations where the person is really struggling, looking through a list of possible skills might be a useful prompt. It can take the pressure off them to 'describe' or name their skills and is often easier to point to a few words on a page – it can initially make the process less personal. We can all forget things as well so a list can help prompt a memory about a comment that was made about the person's skills. Similarly, when we've done this in groups, we've asked each person to share one of their skills and this often prompts people to add something they've heard from others to their own list.

Have a readymade list of skills that you can fall back on if you absolutely need to. For your own purposes keep this up to date with ideas that you get from working with other people – it makes it more real and you can then talk about these coming from people who have been in a similar situation.

IN THE SESSION ...

Ask if it would be helpful to share some skills that other people have named. Then you can use the lists that you've already generated. It might help to make these intriguing to look at. Think about how you lay them out so they're not just boring lists of words.

And if all else fails ...

IN THE SESSION ...

Although it sounds counterintuitive, if you both get really stuck, you can make a list of skills that the person absolutely doesn't have.

As they make the list you can have a bit of fun (if you have a good enough relationship) looking at each thing and thinking about whether it's really true that they *have absolutely never in all their lives* used that skill. Usually that's not the case and the situation proves to be slightly less bleak than they feared.

Examples may include determination, building supportive relationships, doing voluntary work, building friendships that matter, being aware of how I impact on other people, being motivated, independent, good at communicating with others, good understanding of my own emotions, kind.

IN THE SESSION ...

Invite the person to transfer these ideas to their recovery ladder.

JR's Story

At the start of the Steps to Recovery work JR would often speak of how they had always coped with difficult times in the past, but that over time these skills and resources had faded away. There was a reality to the fact that, with age, many of the skills that JR was referring to had changed, such as their physical ability to keep active around the house as a distraction to feeling low. However, what had not changed was JR's problem solving skills. These were still intact, but just not able to be expressed in quite the same way. Within this session JR was able to see that they could still solve the problem of their garden being untidy (which was making JR feel upset and embarrassed), but instead of getting outside and doing it all themselves, JR was able to look up someone who could help tidy the garden. JR had still 'problem solved', but in a different way.

The person's resources

The next step is to think about the resources that are available to the person. This is really important for two reasons. We often underestimate how many resources we have at our disposal and looking at what there is can help us work out a plan – including finding ways to strengthen those resources. It can also be a very fruitful conversation to help people think broadly about what resources

Don't take our word for it!

'I feel better just spending this hour here. ... Just putting it all down and seeing it out there keeps it making sense and shows me I can do it.' (James)

they have access to. What it should never be though is a Pollyanna 'positive thinking' conversation where you try to repaint someone's life into being something it isn't. It's much more powerful to identify two really strong resources that the person can actually use and is willing to draw on than to gloss over social problems, draw up a long but untrue list, and leave the person feeling somehow inadequate because they can't see how they could use these things.

There are numerous ways you might think about resources and people will often think about 'things' and money. But it's also important to think about the people around you, the places you work and live, the technology you can access and anything else that is available for you to draw on.

IN THE SESSION ...

Explain that you are going to think together about resources that are available to support their recovery.

- Make sure that the wide range of what this might mean is clear to you both.
- Once you've thought about those categories, possibly using Figure 5.2, encourage them to draw out the headings and then think about what is available to them under each.

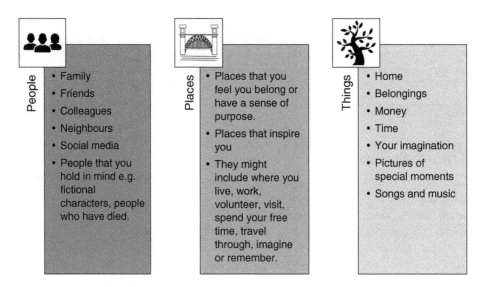

Figure 5.2   Different types of resource

Each item then has a number of characteristics, which brings us back to the fallacy that something has to be 100% positive before it can be included. Every resource has strengths and limitations and there may only be certain elements that the person will choose to make use of. For example, under *people* you might list 'family'. The characteristics of that family might be that they are simultaneously loving, critical, fun and erratic. How you might make use of that resource might need some thought. The type and timing of a request for help and the way it is asked (or of which family member) might make all the difference to the outcome. There is no point in glossing over or idealising a situation. Being able to talk about the subtleties is much more helpful. Figures 5.3 and 5.4 show how this breaks down for one of us in relation to where we live.

Part 2: Doing something different (positive risk taking)

The very concept of *positive risk taking* is ambiguous in how it is interpreted and used in mental health services. The term itself is in some ways part of the problem and some people really struggle with putting 'positive' and 'risk' together in the same term. We deliberated for a long time about whether to use it and decided that the term is so universal that we needed to be clear about how our thoughts linked with common terminology in mental health services.

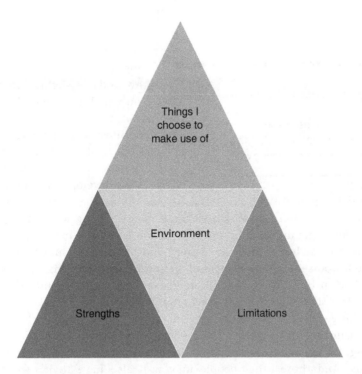

Figure 5.3   The characteristics of where people spend time or live

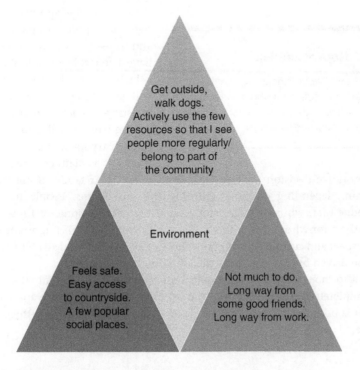

Figure 5.4   One of our 'maps'

If there is only one session where you spend time beforehand talking with colleagues then this is it. Make sure that you understand how the service thinks about this concept and what this means for you and the person you are working with.

When we use it we mean trying new things that have the potential to help you grow and are slightly uncomfortable. To genuinely learn something new, you (and possibly people around you) have to be out of your comfort zone, but not too much and preferably with support. Vygotsky, a psychologist in the early 1900s, developed the idea of the zone of proximal development (Wenzel, 2017). He was talking about being supported by someone with more mastery of a skill, whereas we're talking about being supported by someone who is genuinely alongside you as you learn (but may have no more mastery of the things being learnt than the learner). But the point about being supported whilst you stretch yourself is important and Vygotsky also saw this as a dynamic process between both people. We're not talking about pushing people into risky situations, or ignoring clear signs that this is too much at this point in time. We're also not talking about making someone do something that would make everyone else's life 'easier', but is totally daunting for the person themselves. It's also rarely just about the person doing something. We are all social animals and we learn best when we are supported by those around us. And those other people may well also have their own anxieties about change.

Note of caution

We've seen very emotive, uncurious arguments where people have become polarised about the potential risks involved in a way that hasn't been helpful to anyone. Mutual respect and listening is key.

We've seen the approach used very positively to support people to try new things and to really grow. In those situations staff have been able to talk about the positive risks that they themselves also take day in and day out. They've reflected on the paternalistic approach of many services and the consequences (real and feared) that may result if trying something different doesn't work out as planned. There has been genuine collaborative decision making with the person, their family if appropriate, and the wider team, depending on how daunting the idea seems. People have been able to acknowledge that, whilst it might not seem a big deal for some of those involved, there may be others for whom this seems a step too far. What's been important has been maintaining respect and curiosity throughout those conversations and an ability to acknowledge, but not be driven by, the emotions the situation has generated.

We've also though seen mental health staff intolerant of the idea that any risk is possible whilst completely failing to reflect on the risks that they actively take and enjoy themselves. Often this is born out of fear but it needs naming so that a more healthy conversation can take place.

So to summarise (Table 5.1), what we're introducing here are conversations about

- something that the person might choose to do;
- that has a 'strong enough' possibility of helping them to learn something or change;
- and is something that matters to them.

And the fact that the person you are working with is going to try something new might mean that you and other people also have to change how you behave. This is important to us. It's about identifying (realistic) challenges that can support the person to achieve a goal that matters to them.

Table 5.1 What positive risk taking is and is not

Positive risk taking is...	Positive risk taking isn't...
Doing something that you have chosen.	Being made to do something you don't want to do.
Doing something, no matter how small it might seem to you or other people, that feels a bit out of your comfort zone.	Doing something just because it frightens you/ only choosing 'big' things to take on.
Doing what you think is important.	Doing something that someone else thinks is important for you.
Doing something that is very clearly linked to what you want to be different.	Doing something that has no clear relationship with your personal goals for growth.
Involving other people – change can be daunting and we all need help.	Being coerced to do something risky while everyone else washes their hands of the situation.

It goes without saying that what seems daunting to one person can seem insignificant to someone else; and that doesn't matter. Recovery, growth and change are individual and idiosyncratic and often not straightforward. And, because of that, there is no rule about what constitutes a positive step into something slightly daunting for each person. It might include developing a new interest, trying something that's not guaranteed to work, deciding to act differently in a new relationship, taking on a new role, saying no to someone/thing, saying yes to someone/thing, speaking up, staying quiet, making a complaint, complimenting someone, complimenting yourself.

By now you should have a really clear shared idea of what the person is trying to achieve and what things have stopped them making that change.

Go back to those goals.

- What small next step could the person take that they have either put off or not dared to think they could try?
- What might the benefits of taking that step be?
- Even if the step doesn't go to plan, what else might come from it e.g. the opportunity to prove you can have a go, the chance for someone else to help, the chance to learn a bit more about what a realistic next step might be.
- Identify one step that the person wants to try this week. Small steps are just as important as large ones so the idea does not have to be huge.

It's important to be specific and realistic e.g. 'This week I will phone the friend that I haven't spoken to in a while and stay on the phone for a minimum of three minutes.'

Examples have included: speak to an old friend, sign up to a dance class, spring clean the back room, make a telephone call I have been putting off, enquire about something I am interested in doing, say no next time someone asks for help.

If you can work out the specifics of the day/time etc. when they will try this different thing, you can reduce the chance that the plan is thrown off course or that they feel underprepared to do it. Going through the specifics of how it will work gives you a chance to identify any potential obstacles or worries and to address them. It also allows you both to think through how realistic the goal is and, if necessary, reduce it for this first step. There is always next week to increase the goal.

Bringing the two parts together and adding to the ladder

Invite the person to add to their ladder with the things that they have learnt about their personal skills and the resources available to them.

Then ask them to identify one step that they want to try this week using Worksheet 5.1 Trying Something New.

And then plan how they will celebrate their success in trying it (regardless of how well it goes). It's easy to lose this step and not 'notice'. But if it was a step worth taking then it's a step worth celebrating.

James' Story

We ended up doing this session in two parts. The section on skills became quite complex and rich and we returned to the positive risk taking section the week after.

Skills

James found this session uncomfortable. He wasn't quick to tell me what skills he had and came up with a fairly limited list of words that seemed to be ones he thought weren't overselling himself. We went through the questions about what other people would say about him and that elicited a few more. I also then asked if I could contribute a few.

The really interesting thing for James was the moment when we talked about where his strengths had taken him. One that he was happy to throw into the pot was decisiveness and determination. That had clearly helped in a number of ways through his life, for example he had created a number of opportunities for himself and his family that 'objectively' should have been out of reach. And he was proud of those achievements and they were a strong part of his narrative about his life and himself.

However, that same decisiveness and determination had also led him to try to take his own life. At a time when things seemed unsolvable, he had fallen back on his greatest strength and the power of that 'skill' now frightened him. It was important then to think about the role that other people play in keeping him well, alongside the other skills he had that balanced his decisiveness. The trick was learning when each skill was needed.

We've talked earlier in the book about not sticking rigidly to the session structure and knowing about the other resources so you can move fluidly through them. At this point James added to the ladder about the things that might trip him up in the future and strategies for dealing with those. We also went back to the chart of the relationships he had around him and thought about the 'me' in the middle (Figure 5.5). It enabled us to have a conversation about the possibility that the 'me' in the middle could at times be bigger and more important than the people around him, i.e. it being okay to look after and think about himself. And then that there were times when 'me' could be smaller and other people in that diagram could play a larger role. That diagram featured heavily again in the 'outsider witness' session with his daughters at the end of our time together.

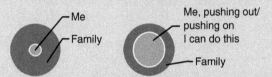

Figure 5.5 How James began to describe that he could be as important a focus as other people

(Continued)

(Continued)

We didn't talk about this in detail until later in our work but the impact of environment and what that gave him access to was a central theme of our work. During our time together James moved from a very isolated village to a small town which was near one daughter and on the other daughter's drive home from work. The move stalled for a while because it got wrapped up in two things:

- saying goodbye to the chapter of life with his wife;
- his pride in his self-determination – the more pressure that came from his family to move as it would be 'good for him', the more he resisted and for a while just refused to consider it. We then went back to the work we had done on his identity and looked at other elements which might be just as, if not more, important to him. Once he had the space to think about what *he* actually wanted, he decided to move.

At a stroke his environment became 'resource rich'. He found the option to work and could go out and meet people every day just by walking round. He could see people coming and going and his daughters could pop in and reassure themselves without being intrusive. And he had a large number of activities going on in the town that he could choose to go to or not. He also had many more visits from his grandchildren who could pop in, and he could tell them to go when he'd had enough because they hadn't come so far in the first place.

Positive risk taking

This was a really well placed session for James and we did this as a stand-alone session. He had made good progress which had been sustained and we were both getting on well. The danger that I could see was that we would drift into being comfortable and not bring up anything challenging.

James' body language was really important in this session. We had already talked about his expressive facial expressions and there was a noticeable change between conversations about his 'progress' as he saw it – the things that he could tangibly see he'd done – and the things that he had been putting off.

When we got to the tasks that he had said he wanted to do but not got to, he looked quite bashful. We began to talk about the paperwork he had been putting off dealing with. It had begun with an offhand comment about a pile of paperwork that he needed to deal with. We looked at his confidence in being able to split it into 'junk' and 'things to deal with' by our next appointment. He said his confidence was 6/10 that he *could* complete it. I asked if he *would* do it and he became ambivalent. I took a step back and asked him to set a goal, however small, that he thought he could (and would) do in the week. He started repeating that he would deal with it but without any firm commitment whilst also saying that he had missed a recent appointment and the letter must have been lost in the pile. I asked what was getting in the way. He then told me that there were actually three piles and he'd tried to deal with mail as it came in but lost control of it. It was also a job his wife would have done.

And so we got into a conversation about the difficulties of clearing things out of the house in preparation for moving (which inevitably included clearing through his wife's belongings) and also taking on jobs that she had previously done. It was a lot of 'moving on' to do in one week.

So we agreed a new goal, to deal with one more piece of paper than typically came through the post. So each day he would file three pieces of mail from any of the piles.

As it turned out, the hard bit was talking about it with me and emotionally processing the meaning of the letters and what 'clearing out' items from the house represented to him and his wife's memory. When James came back for the next session he had gone through all the piles of mail and moved on to other items in the house.

Worksheet 5.1   Trying Something New

This week I am going to:

....

....

....

Some examples might include – speak to an old friend, sign up to a dance class, spring clean the back room, make a telephone call I have been putting off, enquire about something I am interested in doing, not apologise for not being able to go to an event I don't want to be at – just politely decline, walk to work a different way and take a real look at what's around me.

These things or people will help me achieve it (including planning for things that might get in the way):

....

....

....

Some examples might include planning time to do the task, not spending too much time dwelling on the task, asking someone I know to support me, finding out information about the thing I am going to do, drawing upon past experience, asking others for advice.

Session 6

Developing and Maintaining Relationships

This session explores the important role that relationships can play in a person's recovery. The exercises encourage the person to consider relationships that are important to them and what they can do to influence, develop and/or maintain these relationships. We also explore possible barriers to forming relationships and how to overcome these.

For this session you will need

- Worksheet 6.1 The Impact on Relationships

- Worksheet 6.2 Barriers to Relationships

- Worksheet 6.3 My Circle of Relationships

- Worksheet 6.4 Nurturing and Maintaining Relationships

Visit https://resources.sagepub.com/stepstorecovery to download

Relationships and mental health

Feeling a connection to others, through good quality relationships, can have a profoundly positive impact on people's mental health and recovery.

IN THE SESSION ...

To introduce this session, it may be helpful to think together about the following:

- As human beings, relationships form part of our daily lives.
- Many people experience good mental health when they have positive relationships with people that are important to them.
- Just as you need to water a plant and give it all the right elements for it to grow, relationships require care and attention in order to be maintained.
- In this session we are going to look at the relationships that are important to you in your recovery and how you can work at influencing, developing/maintaining these relationships.

Research suggests that having a friend who is happy and lives close by can increase happiness by as much as 25%. Similar results have been found for cohabitant spouses (8%), siblings (14%) and next-door neighbours (34%) (Mental Health Foundation, 2016).

There is a lot of research that consistently shows that those who feel lonely or socially isolated tend to experience higher rates of depression and other mental health difficulties (Smith & Victor, 2018). This will not come as a surprise to most people; the notion of needing to connect with others forms part of many cultures and human development from the beginning of life. What is perhaps less understood is the reciprocal impact that mental health can have on feeling or becoming isolated/lonely.

So many of the people we have had the pleasure of supporting have spoken of how their psychological distress can create 'barriers' to important relationships in their lives. If left unaddressed, these barriers can lead to an increasing sense of loneliness and isolation, which can increase symptoms of mental health difficulties. As Figure 6.1 illustrates, loneliness/ isolation and mental health difficulties can affect each other.

Figure 6.1   The impact on relationships

| IN THE SESSION ... |

As this is such an important point to discuss at the start of the session, we have included the above diagram as Worksheet 6.1 which you may like to use to start the conversation.

Barriers to forming and maintaining relationships

In order for the person to consider how they may develop and maintain close relationships as part of their recovery, it is first important to name and consider some of the potential barriers or factors that can get in the way of relationships with others. It is worth mentioning at this point that many people may not have considered 'barriers' to forming or maintaining relationships, so it can be useful to hold in mind some examples to prompt the conversation. To help with this we have summarised some barriers that have arisen for people we know.

- Confidence to engage with others.
- Worrying that they will not have anything to offer in the relationship.
- Fear of not being 'wanted' or being rejected in relationships.
- Lacking motivation to make contact with others.
- Just simply 'drifting' apart from others (and not realising the distance that this has created).
- Finding that their mental health difficulties change their perceived role in a relationship e.g. not feeling or being perceived as able to help the other person in the same way as before.
- Worrying about other people's judgements e.g. '... *I often run back inside the house before the neighbour can speak to me, as I am afraid that he will see how unwell I am and think poorly of me'.*

| JR's Story |

Whilst engaging with the Steps to Recovery work JR experienced some physical health difficulties, which left them in considerable pain and discomfort. This also meant that JR was unable to do as many activities with their partner as they had done in the past. Being able to 'get out and about' was important to JR, not least because it offered mental stimulation, but this would often allow time for JR and their partner to talk. When remaining at home for long periods of time, with ongoing pain and discomfort, JR found that they did not want to 'burden' their partner by talking about their problems. At the same time JR's partner did not want JR to feel the need to talk if they didn't want to, and so 'the dark mist' (of depression) caused feelings of distance from each other.

Feelings of isolation also increased when JR found it hard to tell their mental health team about how they were struggling with feelings of low mood. Having made steady progress in their recovery JR felt 'ashamed' that they may be experiencing a relapse in their mental health. JR also noticed thoughts such as 'they should be spending their time with people who need it more than me' and 'I don't want to be a burden to them'. JR and their clinician started to write some of these barriers down as 'bricks in the wall', that were creating distance in close relationships.

IN THE SESSION ...

Taking the metaphor of barriers as being bricks in a wall between the person and others, use Worksheet 6.2 and ask the person if they can think of any barriers that 'get in the way' or stop them from having relationships with people that are important to them.

- Remember this may not just be related to their mental health or even to them. *All* barriers are important to consider.

Identifying important relationships

If the person you are working with is having difficulty identifying relationships other than friends and family, it can be helpful to ask them to describe all the people they may meet/interact with in a week, month, or year. This has often helped us to identify relationships that are at a glance brief encounters, but on further discussion quite important e.g. for Jenny, speaking to the bus drivers each day during her daily commute became a helpful means of having a problem-free chat.

When we ask people to think about the relationships that they have in their life, their thoughts often move towards family members or friends. For most people these are indeed the most important relationships. However, there is a risk in just stopping there and not taking the time to really consider the many connections and relationships that people often have. Meaningful connections and relationships can take many forms and may be meaningful for a whole host of reasons. Figure 6.2 illustrates some of the meaningful relationships that we have come across.

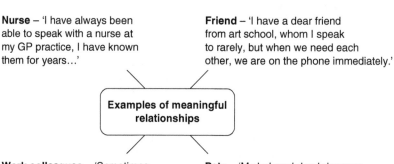

Nurse – 'I have always been able to speak with a nurse at my GP practice, I have known them for years…'

Friend – 'I have a dear friend from art school, whom I speak to rarely, but when we need each other, we are on the phone immediately.'

Examples of meaningful relationships

Work colleagues – 'Sometimes I speak more with a couple of work colleagues than I do with my partner, as we spend so much time together.'

Pets – 'My beloved dog brings me companionship and love, sometimes more than anyone else in my life.'

Figure 6.2   Examples of meaningful relationships from people we've worked with

The next step is to think about the idea that not all relationships hold the same value. This is often difficult for people to acknowledge even to themselves. But if you have limited personal resource, energy or time, you can only invest it in some relationships. The problem with not acknowledging the relative value you place on relationships is that you end up investing a lot in the relationships that shout loudest or demand most. And they might well not be the relationships that matter most to you.

IN THE SESSION ...

Circles of Relationships. Using Worksheet 6.3 talk with the person about:

- all of the relationships that are important in their life and that will be important in their recovery;
- people closer to the centre would be very important. As you get further towards the edge people may still be important but play a less significant role;
- outside of the circle they can put people who they do not want to be involved in their recovery.

When completing this exercise, be curious, whilst also remembering that some relationships may feel 'okay' to speak about, whereas others may not. This may be the first time in a long time (if ever) that the person has spoken about how they feel about certain relationships in their life, so it is important to keep checking in with them on how they are feeling during the activity. If the person is engaging well with the activity, some helpful questions to ask about each relationship may be:

Sometimes people may have relationships that are very important to them, but who may not be important to their recovery. For example, they may love their parents dearly and be very close, but not wish to have them part of their recovery as they often get into arguments. You can always do this exercise twice – one for those close to them and one for those important in their recovery.

- What made you place that person there (pointing to the position on the circles)?
- What is it about your relationships with that person that will be helpful in your recovery?
- What is it about your relationships with that person that may be unhelpful in your recovery (for those that are placed outside the circles on the diagram)?
- Are there any relationships on the diagram that may move closer or further away as your recovery progresses?

Nurturing relationships

So far, the session has explored the impact that mental health can have on relationships, possible barriers to meaningful relationships, and which relationships are important in the person's recovery. In this last part of the session, the focus is on helping the person to consider what steps they and others can take to help nurture these important relationships as part of their recovery.

There is a lot of research that details the factors that can help to foster and maintain relationships such as reciprocity (exchanging things with others for mutual benefit). However, ultimately every relationship is unique. It's hard to stress this point enough. We have often been amazed at what people state makes *that* relationship work. For some, spending lots of time together helps to foster a sense of closeness, whereas for others this can lead to 'bickering' and more distance in the relationship. Not only do different relationships therefore require different 'things', but they may also require a different approach depending on the current circumstances.

Given that every relationship requires a different approach at a different point in time, the only way to truly help the person consider this is to take each relationship in turn. Referring to the previous exercise (circle of relationships), invite the person to choose one relationship to focus on for this next exercise. If they are finding it hard to choose, you may suggest starting with those that they have placed closest to the centre, i.e. the ones which they have rated as being most important in their recovery.

IN THE SESSION ...

To introduce the final activity of the session, ask the person to choose one of the relationships that they felt would be important in their recovery. Then explain that you would like to help them to consider how they would like to develop or maintain this important relationship.

Worksheet 6.4 can be used to help with this conversation.

When people are experiencing difficulties in their mental health, they may find it particularly hard to generate ideas on how to develop the relationship, so having some helpful questions, such as the ones below, may generate conversation:

1.   Can you remember a time when you felt your relationship to this person was in 'a good place'?
2.   How did you and the other person interact with each other when the relationship was like that?

3. How would you like this relationship to fit in with your life at this time?
4. What do you think the other person would be looking for from you in this relationship?
5. What would you need to do to connect with this person?

Adding to the ladder

IN THE SESSION ...

To end the session, encourage the person to summarise the three areas you have explored and to capture this within the recovery ladder:

1. Relationships that are important in their recovery.
2. Barriers/things that can get in the way of these relationships.
3. What they can do to nurture and maintain these relationships.

James' Story

This was such a big part of James' recovery. It mattered intensely to him that his family treated him normally and didn't feel sorry for him. In all our early sessions we looked at the chart showing all the people he cared about and hoped still cared about him (Figure 6.3). He coloured each section in one colour as he gradually saw and developed confidence again in those relationships as being safe again. We also made sure that it was alright to colour some in as unsafe. Most relationships started unsafe to some extent and gradually were replaced by safe (Figure 6.4). One relationship oscillated up and down in colour and eventually stayed mainly unsafe. This was okay. It was a key point where James started to show some of his decisive nature and decide what he wanted rather than worrying about what he ought/not to do. Being upfront about the non-linear progress of recovery and acknowledging the ups and downs in what was, for a while, a very important relationship, was important in ensuring James could talk about a relationship that his family were not comfortable with. We also had a very funny conversation where he told me that the mental health team were currently quite close to him in the circles but that he was hoping eventually we would be much further out. Not that he didn't like us he explained, just that he really didn't want to need us anymore.

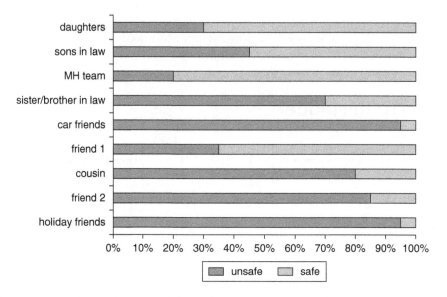

Figure 6.3   Feeling unsafe and safe with relationships: Session 2

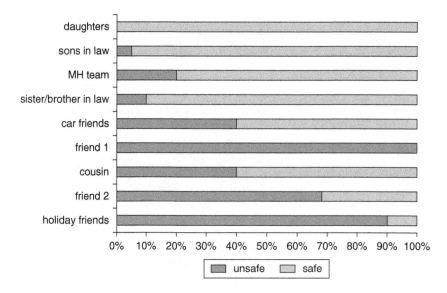

Figure 6.4   Feeling unsafe and safe with relationships: Session 6

Worksheet 6.1   The Impact on Relationships

Mental health difficulties can have a very big impact on relationships and if not addressed, leave some people feeling isolated or lonely.

What kind of mental health factors may impact on relationships?

| Mental health difficulties |

⟺

| Loneliness & isolation from important relationships |

Worksheet 6.2   Barriers to Relationships

Can you think of any barriers that 'get in the way' or stop you from having relationships with people that are important to you?

Some people find it helpful to write each barrier on a separate brick to see them laid out. Others have done lists or spider diagrams. Just do what feels right for you.

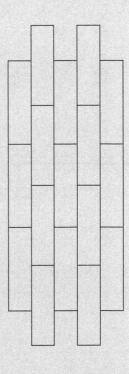

Worksheet 6.3   My Circle of Relationships

In the diagram below you can write down all of the relationships that are important in your life and that will be important in your recovery.

People closer to the centre are very important in your recovery. As you get further towards the edge people may still be important, but play a less significant role.

You can also list on the outside of the circle people who you do not want to be involved in your recovery.

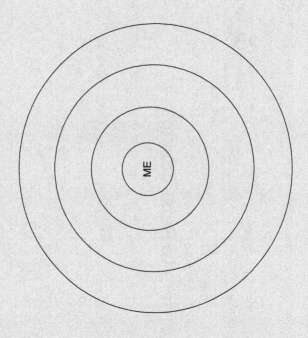

Worksheet 6.4   Nurturing and Maintaining Relationships

Just as a plant needs key elements to grow and thrive, relationships require certain conditions to develop and be maintained.

Using the metaphor of relationships as a precious plant:

What would bring sunshine to the relationships (what kind of things would be nice to put in and get out of the relationship)?

....

....

....

....

What would give the relationships water (what would the relationship need on a regular basis to survive)?

....
....

What would allow the relationships to be protected from storms (what may prevent it being harmed by outside forces)?

....
....

How can you make sure the relationship has strong roots (what will allow the relationship to feel safe and secure)?

....
....

Session 7

Returning to Recovery

This session explores the ways in which people may identify signs that they are experiencing difficulties in their recovery. It then helps you both put together some ideas about the things that the person and others can do which might be helpful.

For this session you will need

*   Worksheet 7.1   If I 'Fall Off' the Ladder I Could ...

Visit https://resources.sagepub.com/stepstorecovery to download

Reviewing the journey so far

Don't take our word for it!

'Don't underestimate the tiny things, this is a journey of small meaningful steps, not a single miracle.' (Molly)

The premise of this whole book is that recovery is not linear. We talked in session 1 about the shape that people often imagine recovery takes and the more wobbly reality for most people. This is a good point to revisit that conversation. Some people will have found that they have made good progress to this point and might even have started to believe that things will be 'different' for them and their recovery will continue on an upward path. It can then come as a shock when things get difficult and a lot of people can internalise this and believe that it is due to something that they have done. Perhaps they believe they didn't 'work hard enough' at the exercises or are being 'punished' for something. It might reinforce a belief they have that things will never work out. Some of these beliefs might be linked to the way that stigma and attitudes towards mental health have affected them and the people they are close to. Remember that you can jump around these resources. If it makes sense to go back to another session such as session 3, then take the time to do so.

IN THE SESSION ...

Take some time at the start of this session to look back over how things have gone so far. Has the path been a surprise, were there any highs and lows, where are they at the moment?

When things don't go to plan

There are numerous words for this experience, which are worth thinking about together e.g. relapse, deterioration, and setback, associated with 'warning signs' and relapse prevention plans.

Some of those words might seem small and inconsequential. But can frame the entire way that an individual (or those around them) interpret mental health and how people live their lives. Our concern about this language is that it tends to give the impression that low periods are something to be 'managed' and 'prevented' and they mimic a lot of the language of physical ill health. If this suits the person you are working with, all well and good. But it's just as important that they find a language that they are comfortable using and sharing in relation to when things are difficult as the language they choose to use about recovery itself. If the words don't feel right for them then it adds another barrier to their ability to talk with others if they need help. Our own view tends to be that periods of feeing rough are part and parcel of being human. Recovery might mean that the ups and downs are less extreme or less frequent but probably not something to be prevented. At its worst, unhelpful language about mental wellbeing can in itself derail someone's recovery.

Alex's Story

Alex had decided that, for her, recovery meant spending more time with her husband doing things that they used to do and having fun together. The implications for her and everyone else were very clear, it was achievable and it made a significant difference to the way they both experienced themselves and their relationship. But as time went on, the pressure (through unspoken assumptions) meant that expectations returned to reducing 'symptoms' which didn't actually bother Alex that much. Gradually the time and focus on the volume and quality of her time with her husband diminished as did her experience of feeling recovered vs 'ill'.

For Alex, a collective understanding by other people of her being 'ill' led to an experience whereby professional input was prioritised and brought with it treatment, 'expert advice', being 'monitored' and being expected to attend multiple appointments with many staff in the service. What she actually wanted, and what had helped her up to this point, was to do less of all those things so that she had time to spend with her husband, and to focus on family and friends. She needed help to find bus and restaurant times and make plans for how to achieve all those things even when she had difficult periods. It would obviously have been possible to balance both sides of that conversation but it needed the service to acknowledge what mattered to her and to give that equal priority in discussions about what happened next.

Some people will only ever experience one episode of mental health difficulties. But as we discussed in session 1, most of us wobble around rather than having a clear linear path from distress to a uniform experience of sustained wellbeing. It's useful to have a plan thought through before we experience difficulties again. And it can be very important that other people know both the signs that might show we're struggling and what they can do to support us. That's what this session takes you through. Worksheet 7.1 gives you some examples of things that people we have worked with have chosen to do.

How do you talk about it?

IN THE SESSION ...

Think about the words that they and others (family, friends, colleagues, media, and services) use to describe the situation where someone experiences another period of mental distress. Don't judge them or overthink it – just scribble down a load of words that come to mind.

If you need some other ideas these are words we've come across (but don't rush to look at them; spend time coming up with their list, not ours):

- Fall back/off
- Revert
- Regress
- Slip
- Relapse
- Deteriorate
- Reoccurrence
- Worsening

IN THE SESSION ...

Go over the words they've listed. Which of those are difficult to hear/use and which does the person feel comfortable using in relation to themselves?

- If they prefer one word, would the people around them know what they are referring to?
- If they wouldn't understand its meaning, make a note of this to come back to later when you talk about how other people can help.

Personal signs that things are not going well

For all of us there are signs that things are not as they should be. They can be very obvious or take us years to notice. They can be clear to other people and yet hidden to ourselves or vice versa. But we all have that signature pattern of signs that things are deteriorating. It's worth spending some time on this. The signs might seem quite inconsequential but be really important and it might need a conversation with someone else to ask them to point out when they've started.

JR's Story

During the course of the Steps to Recovery work, JR experienced a decline in their mental health. This was a very difficult time for JR and brought about feelings of 'letting others down', 'failure' and wondering if they would ever return to recovery. While no one would ever wish to experience a decline in their mental health, it did present both JR and the therapist with an opportunity to explore in 'real time' what the indicators of change were. Remaining brave and courageous had always been a core part of JR's identity, but at this difficult time, these values started to 'get in the way' of feeling able to ask for help. These values were also leading JR to sometimes push themselves to cope without taking medication, which had been very helpful to them in the past, but was now contributing to their distress.

By spending time talking about this observation JR and the therapist were able to add the following relapse indicators to the ladder:

1. Wanting to cope without medication – trying to avoid taking pain relief.
2. Trying to cope on my own – not asking for help and not being open about my feelings.

IN THE SESSION ...

Take a piece of paper and split it into two columns. Put these headings (or similar) at the top of one column each:

- How I might notice when I am finding things difficult?
- How might others know that I am finding things difficult?

The reason for splitting this into the two columns is to start to think about both what the person's internal experience is and how they are perceived by the outside world. These can be very different. Someone can feel flat and lacking that spark, yet show nothing different to people around them. On the other hand we can sometimes feel

Use the person's choice of words to head up these columns (not ours). This is their resource. Our suggestions are just that. They are no more important than anyone else's.

that we are fine as we get on with living day to day but others notice the slight change in how we greet them, how we dress, our enthusiasm for a piece of work etc., which flag to them that all might not be well, long before we've noticed.

IN THE SESSION ...

Now spend some time together thinking about how the person would answer these questions for themselves. Ask about specific periods where this has happened, or times when things have not gone well and the signs they notice in themselves when they feel under stress or pressure.

Perhaps also think about when you have both seen other people become unwell – do any of the signs that you have both noticed in others offer some possibilities that are relevant to the person you are working with?

IN THE SESSION ...

The next question to think about together is how other people would answer this, i.e. how they would know if the person was becoming unwell? Those around us often have a different insight into the small signs that initially indicate something might be wrong.

Examples of what other people might notice include:

- Changes in the way you talk about things
- Changes in the way you feel or how you describe yourself
- Spending more time on your own
- Looking a bit less smart than usual
- Becoming more distant
- Losing your appetite
- Become more suspicious and wary
- Not keeping track of conversations

The list is endless and very personal.

What to do when things do start to go wrong

Do this for yourself before you start a conversation with another person about it. You'll become more aware of the small, very personal things that indicate your own wellbeing. That will help you be more attuned to the way the other person talks about themselves and the often easy to miss changes in their posture, expression, speech that those around them, including you, will pick up even when they don't.

Noticing that something is wrong is the first step. But, unless there is a plan for what to do next, just knowing that something is wrong can feel overwhelming. By now you will hopefully both have some fairly good ideas about what is/not helpful. All the key points from each session will now be on the ladder and should give you some food for thought about what would help. Sometimes it's as useful to tell people what won't help because people can, with the best of intentions, make things worse.

You will have also spent time together thinking about who is important to the person and how those relationships can be nurtured and maintained. Putting all these things together can give you a very clear set of ideas about who can do what to help the person without taking over. But don't assume that any of them know what they could do. Part of this session's task is to think about how the person will talk through these plans with the people that are important to them, the potential barriers they might face, and how they can work round them.

IN THE SESSION ...

Spend some time thinking through what the person and those around them can do when they notice these signs.

- How will the other people know that this would be helpful?
- There are some ideas on Worksheet 7.1 if you need some inspiration but, as ever, their own ideas will be better than ours.

Adding to the ladder

IN THE SESSION ...

Invite the person to add the key signs that they or other people might notice that indicate things are becoming difficult.

- How will they talk to the people that they trust about this?
- Identify the most helpful thing/s that they or other people could do in this situation.

Preparing for the final session

The next session is the final one and is the session with the outsider witness. You will need to make sure that you are prepared for this so that you can concentrate on the people in the room rather than worrying about the purpose of having someone else with you.

Read the content of session 8 until you are comfortable with it. And take time at the end of session 7 to make sure that the person you are working with is also comfortable with what will happen and why the session is structured as it is.

IN THE SESSION ...

Check that the person understands the purpose and structure of the next session. Make sure that the person who they have identified as their 'outsider witness' is able to come to the session and also has an idea of how the session will work.

James' Story

James had a couple of significant difficult periods during our work together and a number of other wobbly periods. These tended to be related to his attempt to end his life and created significant anxiety for him, his family, the team and us. They were often related to

- a sense of shame and fear of what people thought;
- some sense that he should have tried harder and not had to rely on other people to help him get well.

These periods were useful in highlighting the things that weren't helpful as much as what was.

It became apparent that there were some things that, once you scratched below the surface, could have a very positive or detrimental impact on his mood. For example, some music was soothing but there were a few specific pieces that he described as using to 'torture' himself. Those pieces rapidly led to late nights, drinking beer and the fear of 'putting upon his family' rearing its head. Gradually he decided not to listen to that music and to not buy any alcohol.

He also rang the crisis team in a state of desperation and realised that they wouldn't rush in and disempower him, that he could trust them, and that there was a value in using them more quickly when he began to be tempted to play that music.

He also began to recognise signs that things weren't 'right'; he began to hide away, be quieter, not talk to visitors and avoid tasks. He would get a sense that things were racing away without him and become more convinced that he needed to do things himself in order to regain control. He would then either withdraw so that other people couldn't take over or give up and 'not feel bothered'. He also noticed that he would start to think he'd *got to* do things rather than wanting to do them.

Again we went back through the material we had already covered. We looked at the section of the ladder about his strengths and who mattered to him. We talked about what happened when he did ask his daughters to think things through with him. It was often okay because once they felt involved and knew what was happening they were able to give him space. It was also help that was invited rather than help that rushed in unasked for. This was the opposite of when he retreated. At those times his daughters panicked and actually took over more because they were worried about him and didn't know why he had withdrawn. This gave him the confidence to ask for help earlier. We also looked at the small regular things he knew kept him feeling better; getting to bed earlier, not listening to sad music, and going outside.

Worksheet 7.1   Examples: If I 'Fall Off' the Ladder I Could ...

- Meet with someone from my recovery team
- Think about what causes me stress and decide how to alleviate it/who could help me
- Tell someone close to me
- Go for coffee with a friend who knows that I just need some time out of the house but don't want to talk
- Spend some time in the garden
- Invite a friend for dinner
- Talk to my GP/a mental health worker
- Do something I enjoy doing that helps me feel better e.g. listen to music, have a bath, go for a walk, speak to my friend
- Do some exercise
- Look at my recovery ladder and see if there are other ideas that I've missed
- Make a conscious decision to say something kind to myself every hour

Session 8

Witnesses to Recovery

Within this session we introduce the process of 'outsider witness', which has its origins in Narrative Therapy. The process of having outsider witness conversations will be broken down into steps, with guidance on how to facilitate a conversation with the person and their 'significant other', to reinforce progress that has been made. There is also guidance on how to plan for continuing the recovery journey after the Steps to Recovery work has finished.

For this session you will need

- Worksheet 8.1 Questions that might help both people reflect on the recovery story

Visit https://resources.sagepub.com/stepstorecovery to download

Other resources for you to refer to:

- Figure 8.2 The layers of 'story-telling'
- Table 8.1 Questions that might help both people reflect on the recovery story

Outsider witness – what is it?

Imagine the scene ... you have just started a new job and you have been working very hard to demonstrate you were the right person for the job. So far you have had little feedback on how you are doing and the inevitable sense of self-doubt creeps in from time to time. As you sit alone, pondering your new role, you unexpectedly hear someone talking just outside the room you are sitting in. Intrigued, you move a little closer to the door that is slightly ajar ... it's your boss! You hear your boss telling a colleague that they are 'very impressed' at how 'committed' you have been since joining the team and how your work is to a 'high standard'. How might you feel?

Hopefully for most, the above scenario would bring about a great sense of pride and other positive emotions. The way in which you heard this may also amplify these feelings; to listen in on a conversation about you, but not directly to you, can often change how you hear it. This concept of 'listening in' on other people's 'retellings' of your story (in this case your 'new job story'), so that you may re-experience the story, is central to the process of outsider witness work. The hope is that by hearing the new story (often referred to as the 'new narrative') in different ways, it becomes richer, deeper, more meaningful and part of the person.

Introducing the session

It's important to take time to carefully introduce this session to both the person and their significant other, who they have chosen to be the outsider witness to the session. Of all the sessions in the Steps to Recovery framework, this is the one that people report as needing the most attention to detail when explaining how it will work. This is because it deliberately follows a process, which is likely to be relatively novel to most people and indeed most practitioners (unless you are familiar with Narrative Therapy practice).

IN THE SESSION ...

The session is typically introduced by explaining the following:

- 'Within the session today we will be taking time to carefully listen to your recovery story, i.e. the journey you have taken so far in your recovery.
- We will start by allowing you to share your recovery story, before then inviting X (the person's outsider witness) to share their reflections on what they have heard about your recovery story/ journey.
- After X (outsider witness) has shared their thoughts and reflections, we will all consider together the themes of what has been heard.'

Seating and positioning in the room

As you might expect, the book has until now not made any reference to seating or positioning during conversation, as whatever feels comfortable for the person and you is best. When facilitating outsider witness conversations however, we have found that it can sometimes be helpful to offer a particular seating arrangement for the session. During the main exercise you will be trying to help the person share their story without interruption, then encourage the outsider witness to do the same, which can be tricky when people are seated side by side.

Seating and positioning can be particularly tricky to change when offering sessions within a person's own home. We find that being open and relaxed about seating from the start (before sitting down) can make the rest of the session run smoothly. Rarely does it come easy to ask people to move when everyone has already sat down, particularly as a guest in their home!

If the person you are working with and their outsider witness are close/comfortable with each other, they are likely to naturally 'chip in' to each other's conversation. The main aim of the activity is to help each person listen carefully to what is being said; feeling the need to 'chip in' or affirm a specific point can be distracting. Therefore, asking the person and their outsider witness to sit slightly apart, so that you can clearly turn to each of them for separate conversations, can be helpful. We are not talking about a huge crevasse of space here and ultimately, we want everyone to feel comfortable. It may be just slightly repositioning the chairs (see Figure 8.1 for an example) or offering everyone a little of their own space for the conversations.

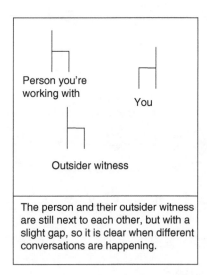

Figure 8.1 Example seating position for outsider witness conversation

Outsider witness – layers of rich story-telling

While the person you have been working with has progressed through the Steps to Recovery framework, they will have been developing their 'recovery story', even if this has not been a conscious process. This might be quite a contrast to previous stories that they have told or had told about them in the past. If we consider their recovery story to be like a cake, there will have been many key ingredients that have gone into the mix; aspects of their identity, understanding of mental health, hope, awareness of skills, relationships etc. At this point in your work, it is hoped that they now have a freshly baked recovery story (it's okay if it needs a little longer in the oven). While the cake is no doubt delightful on its own, what better way to make it even richer than by adding extra layers. As Figure 8.2 demonstrates, each time the recovery story is told and heard by the person, their outsider witness and you, the more layers to the cake are added and who doesn't love a multi-layered cake!

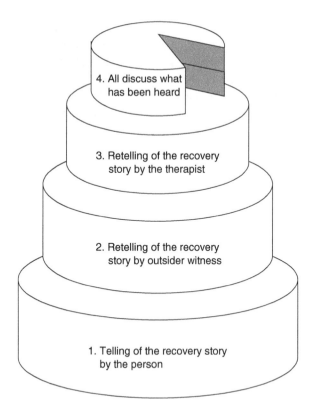

Figure 8.2   The layers of 'story-telling'

Within the outsider witness exercise, the central aim is to help the person connect with their unique recovery story. The process to the exercise is as follows:

Step 1 – Encourage the person to share their story of recovery since starting the Steps to Recovery framework.

Step 2 – After the person has finished speaking, thank them, then turn to their outsider witness and ask them to share with you, their thoughts and reflections about what they have just heard.

Step 3 – After the outsider witness has finished speaking, thank them, then reflect a summary of what you have noticed or what has stood out for you from what has been said by them both.

Step 4 – Allow for a more general conversation from everyone about what has been heard, ensuring that the person you have been working with gets time to strengthen the important elements of their new story.

Table 8.1 has some key questions to use when encouraging the person and the outsider witness to reflect on the recovery story. You will notice that some of these are deliberately similar in tone, to try and help connect some key themes to the recovery story. These have also been added in Worksheet 8.1 for quick reference.

Table 8.1

Questions for the person	Questions for the outsider witness
How would you describe your recovery journey since we started the sessions?	What was it like for you to hear (the person) tell their recovery story?
What changes have you noted?	How would you describe (the person's) recovery journey since they started the sessions?
What things have felt most important in your recovery journey?	What changes have you noted?
Has (the problem – insert the person's description of the problem) changed since starting the Steps to Recovery sessions?	What have you noticed about how (the person) manages (the problem name)?
What surprised you most along the way?	What surprised you most along the way?
How has your recovery journey impacted on others?	How has (person's name) recovery journey impacted on others?
Has anyone else noticed aspects of your recovery journey?	Where do you imagine (the person) going in the future with their recovery?

An example of bringing this together from the three perspectives

---

Alice's Story

'When I began the Steps to Recovery sessions with you (therapist), I must be honest, I wasn't sure that it could change how low I was feeling. As we talked about my mental health I realised that for such a long time now, I had believed that I was the problem. I hated myself for being that way and how it affected those around me. It felt very strange to give the problem a name ("the doubter"), but in a funny way this was helpful. As we had more sessions, I started to realise that I'm a good wife, a good mother and caring person who can do things when I don't listen to "the doubter". When I stopped trying to do "everything" all of the time, but focused on spending time with my son there seemed to be a bit of a change ...'

Outsider witness (Alice's husband) reflections

'... Alice has always been hard on herself and thinks that she is letting people down. It never seemed to matter what we would say to her, she would always find a way of blaming herself for things that happened. It's so nice to hear her talking about herself as "good". She is an amazing wife and mum to our son, but it's the first time I've ever heard her say it. Our son has noticed a change too. Instead of running around trying to do everything for everyone, she seems to spend more time talking and doing things with us both ...'

Practitioner's reflections

'It sounds as though there has been a big shift in how Alice understands the problem – as being something separate to her. Whenever "the doubter" was around it sounds as though it stopped Alice seeing the many good parts of herself. I hope that Alice can hear that these "good parts" have always been there, as Mick (husband) pointed out. It must be nice to not be spending so much time "running around" trying to appease "the doubter". It certainly sounds as though Alice's son has noticed this to be a big change that has allowed more quality time with his Mum ...'

Future recovery plans

As we highlighted at the beginning of the book, recovery may be best thought of as a process rather than a specific destination. Hopefully, the outsider witness activity will help clarify for the person where they currently are in their recovery process/journey, which leads us into thinking of the next steps.

IN THE SESSION ...

Consider using these questions to prompt the person in thinking about their future recovery steps:

- Are there any parts of the Steps to Recovery framework you would like to revisit? If so, who would you like to do this with?
- Who might you need to recruit to help keep the recovery going?
- How would you like to record the recovery ladder?
- Where may you keep your recovery ladder?
- Would you like to share your recovery ladder with others, so that they can help you use aspects of this in the ongoing recovery process? If so, who and why?

There is, perhaps, a temptation at this stage in the recovery framework to look for 'clear plans' and goals for future recovery, to ensure the person holds on to the progress so far. However, the unique nature of each person's journey to this point will inevitably mean that for some 'this is it ...' and they just need to hold on to the experience they have had so far, while for others, 'there is a long way to go ...'. Both positions and anything in-between should be acknowledged and explored. For those who feel that they have reached an acceptable position in their recovery process and they no longer require ongoing 'sessions' to explore the Steps to Recovery framework, it can be helpful to spend a little bit of time considering how they will hold on to that which they have found meaningful.

Documenting and storing recovery ladders

We have encountered the same question from mental health professionals on several occasions when it comes to documenting the person's recovery ladder – 'but where does it go in the clinical records?' The answer we always give is 'where does the person want it to go?' Encouraging the person to take ownership of their recovery ladder is so core to the philosophy of the Steps to Recovery framework, that we make every effort for this to be their decision.

A core element of this is the daily habits that they can build to maintain their wellbeing. Even if they don't hold on to the whole ladder, we would encourage you to think together about an easy way of holding in mind what helps on a daily basis and what to put in place as soon as things start to feel difficult. For one of us, the mantra when our mood dips is 'get outside, take some time away from people, drink some water, do some small exercise, and do something tiny towards whatever feels overwhelming'.

We have found that for many individuals this leads into conversations about where they are going to keep their recovery ladder and who they may like to share it with. In contrast, some individuals may feel that there are certain aspects of the Steps to Recovery framework that they would like to revisit. This may be particularly true when certain aspects of their life, which were explored in the framework, have changed e.g. they may have recently had a loss or change in a significant relationship. Being able to consider the need to revisit or explore a certain session topic is just as important as the person stating that they feel a natural end to the sessions. Ultimately it shows that the person is taking time to consider what they need, for their recovery, at this moment in time.

James' Story

This session took us a long time to organise and is a lesson in getting it set up early on. Trying to work round everyone's commitments was quite complicated. But it was so much fun. All the preparation that we had done together meant that I knew what he had been worried about so I could support him to talk things through.

James' daughters both attended and they were able to talk about when they had each struggled with first the death of his wife/their mother and then his attempt to end his life and subsequent admission. They had the courage to talk about the ripple effects of his struggles on the rest of the family and their genuine determination to help. This ended up not being the stigmatising and alienating experience that I think James had initially feared. His daughters described it as a domino that knocked them all over and that some took longer to stand up again than others. That was why some had taken longer to reconnect with James; not because they didn't want to, or anything to do with what they thought about him/what he had done, but because they were all dealing with their own emotions. This was far more powerful than a bland reassurance that it was all okay and not to worry about the impact on other people. Of course other people were affected, they cared about him. But it enabled some really significant worries to be aired and worked through (and laughed about). It also contextualised why they were not always easily able to 'leave him be' because they were also worried and grieving. Talking about their shared experiences also highlighted that his feelings didn't need to be pathologised and weren't an inevitable sign of crisis to be 'reacted to'.

The session also gave us a chance to talk about the ladder (Figure 8.3). James wasn't someone who went back to it regularly. Knowing it was there was helpful and gave him the knowledge that he had the skills to cope. But he didn't always want to 'rummage about in the past'. So we were able to consolidate the value of holding on more proactively to the positive bits of the ladder. Having his daughters know about the existence of the ladder and where it was in the house, meant that they could access it if they needed to and at least knew it was there if they wanted to ask James about it.

As often happens, the session was quite moving. There were tears and that was okay and normal. No one was putting on a front and that was great.

We reflected on how he could now talk about things and smile rather than showing the anxiety in his face as he had in previous sessions. His ability to sit in silence and think rather than give pressured answers gave me confidence that things had changed.

With the problems of getting this session arranged it would have been tempting to say that we could end without getting the family together. We would have missed a very key part of the process. Having everyone in the room consolidated the progress that James had made by giving him the opportunity to hear what others had observed in his recovery. It also gave the daughters a chance to reflect on their concerns and think through with him, the changes that he had made and his confidence that things were qualitatively different.

Watching James listen to his daughters' comments on the changes they had seen in him was lovely. This wasn't something he would have naturally sought out (he would have naturally kept things to himself) but it was powerful to hear them reflecting on the changes for him and the family. It amplified how far he had come and how far away the admission now seemed. For James, who was often focused on what 'he' needed to do next, it was a useful breather to look back at how far he had come and the role other people could play without overwhelming him.

The unique aspects that make up who I am:

A combination of sheer determination, concern for others, special capacity to make friends, and love for my family. I am proud of my reputation for keeping my word.

Witnesses to my recovery:

Daughters

When things wobble I can:

Take a step back and think and talk to other people.
Use my determination.
Remember how much change I am capable of making.
Keep seeing people.

The changes I've already made:

Tried things been honest about what's worked.
Set new goals.
Got things clear in my own mind/set my own priorities.
Started a new chapter and begun clearing things out.
Decided where to live.
Reached out to other people.

The skills I have and things I can draw on:

Determination, communications, charm, crafty
Cooking and DIY. Willing to have a go.
Common sense. Listen to other people.
Make friends easily. Sense of humour.
My experience of working from the age of 10.

These things give me hope that I can recover:

I feel different.
Other people see a change in me.
There are a lot of people that matter to me and love me.
I can imagine a future that is meaningful and enjoyable – for me.

Barriers – things that can get in the way:

Distance I live from them.

Withdrawing from them when I feel under pressure.

I can do the following to maintain these relationships:

Decide to move

Actively contact them at regular intervals so that they feel safe and don't overwhelm me.

These things can make me feel worse:

Going through wife's stuff – need to do it a bit at a time.
Sitting doing nothing and thinking about the past – need to get up.
The winter and not being able to get out – moving to a new town will help this as people will be so close.
Falling out with people/not knowing where I am with them – make sure I spend time with people so I know how things are.

Figure 8.3   James' Recovery Ladder

Worksheet 8.1   Questions that might help both people reflect on the recovery story

Questions for the person	Questions for the outsider witness
How would you describe your recovery journey since we started the sessions?	What was it like for you to hear (the person) tell their recovery story?
What changes have you noted?	How would you describe (the person's) recovery journey since they started the sessions?
What things have felt most important in your recovery journey?	What changes have you noted?
Has (the problem – insert the person's description of the problem) changed since starting the Steps to Recovery sessions?	What have you noticed about how (the person) manages (the problem name)?
What surprised you most along the way?	What surprised you most along the way?
How has your recovery journey impacted on others?	How has (person's name) recovery journey impacted on others?
Has anyone else noticed aspects of your recovery journey?	Where do you imagine (the person) going in the future with their recovery?

Evaluating the Recovery Journey

This chapter explores the tricky issue of evaluating such a personal and idiosyncratic process. Potential ways of approaching it with each person as well as ideas for navigating organisational issues are discussed.

Resources for you to refer to

How do you evaluate something so personal?

If there is one area that occupies a lot of our work time it's the thorny issue of how to demonstrate in mental health services that an intervention has made a difference. This chapter spends time thinking about each of the issues that may be relevant to you and the context in which you work.

When we invest a significant amount of time, effort and emotion into something we all want to know if it's worked. Some things are very obvious and it's clear to you and to other people that change has occurred. But other things are much more complex and less easy to 'track'.

If you had spent months trying to lose weight you would want to know if it had been worth the effort. On the face of it, body weight should be fairly easy to track. You can see it and feel it, as can other people. But even then most people use objective measures of their weight to track their progress, use that feedback and change where they put their effort week by week. Weight loss highlights a number of issues about measuring progress that are worth highlighting before we carry on and are described in Table 9.1.

Table 9.1   Thinking about the elements of evaluation

Key issue	Why it matters	Example
Goal setting Do you know what you're trying to change? What will it look like when you get there?	Knowing what the goal is means that you can work out the best way of seeing how you're doing.	*'I want to lose 10 pounds'* might be a very different goal to *'I want to feel better about myself.'*
Know your baseline How are things now? You need to know where you are compared to where you want to get.	This helps you know how you're doing or how much will need to change. It can also be difficult to remember how things were so you lose a sense of how much progress you've made.	*'I'm 11 stone now. When I've been 10 stone in the past I've felt better and was able to keep to that weight.'*
Be prepared to change your goal Sometimes you achieve a goal only to realise that wasn't the problem in the first place.	Sometimes goals need to change and it can be hard to realise you've put a lot of effort into something only to realise it didn't really matter.	*'I still feel rubbish.'* It might be that getting fit is more important than losing weight in itself. Or it might be that the real issue is something completely different.

Key issue	Why it matters	Example
Know when to change tack Good measures, clarity about your goal and involving other people should also help flag up when something isn't working.	Our tendency is to do the same thing with more effort when it initially doesn't work. Sometimes though we have to change what we're doing.	*'I'm not losing weight on this cabbage diet as quickly as I thought I would. I'd better eat even more cabbage.'* Or maybe try something more balanced.
Know when to slow down Fast isn't always better. Don't let the measure become the priority – the goal is whatever you're working on. The goal isn't to see your measure change as fast as possible.	It can be exciting to see that we are making progress but sometimes this takes over and we lose perspective. Although this might seem like the quickest way to achieve our goal, the long-term consequences can be damaging.	*'I'm losing so much weight, if I eat even less I'll lose weight even faster.'* The problem is that this weight loss may well not be sustained and might make you ill along the way.

So for any change:

- You need a clear goal – that matters to you and is fairly realistic. The thing you measure should be very directly linked to that goal.
- You need to know where you are now – so you can see what the change will entail and so that you can celebrate how far you've come.
- You need to be able to check as you go that the goal is the right one. If your 'measures' are all positive but you still feel awful, then either the goal or the measures are wrong.
- Equally, the goal might be a really good one but the route you're trying might not get you there. If the measures really are linked to what you want to achieve but, despite lots of effort, they're not shifting, then perhaps you need a new route.
- Don't get seduced into thinking that the measure is the most important thing. Your wellbeing is the most important thing. And doing that slowly might be better long term than the short-term 'hit' of seeing the numbers change rapidly.

Making your own measures

As recovery is so personal, it can be a real bonus to develop your own ways of gauging the person's progress. James had pie charts and percentages. Other people have had lines, shapes, specific words that represented stages of recovery/wellbeing, and colours. Make sure

Don't take our word for it!

'Sometimes I've not seen the point of the exercise but once we've done them they've always made sense – I've learnt a lot.' (James)

you have some sense together of what the end points on each scale are so that you have a shared idea of what the person is aiming for e.g. is it 100% perfection or a more realistic but settled point of well-being? Try to anchor a few other points so that you can chart the stages along the way. Otherwise for example, moving from 0 to 80% can feel like a vast ocean and it's easy to be overly swayed by specific recent incidents rather than keeping a broader perspective on the progress they have made.

For James our benchmarks were:

- 100% would mean regularly going abroad in the camper van, meeting new friends, and having a hobby which he did regularly and he would feel he had a purpose in life.
- 75% would mean he felt happier, he was getting away in the van occasionally, and on his bike each week. He would be spending time with 'people that matter'; seeing a range of family members each week (not just his daughters) and seeing at least one friend once a week.
- 35% was how he was when we started work – not using the van or bike, rarely seeing friends but some contact with family.

The other thing to discuss together is how often they will chart their progress. Some people manage to reflect on progress in each session and keep an overarching view. Other people need to make a note each day of how things are so that they don't get knocked off course by one low day.

And it doesn't all need to be numbers. Going back to the idea of keeping a note of changes in language etc., some of the evaluation will come in how the person talks about themselves, the work and the future. About half way through the sessions when I asked James how he was finding the exercises he said; 'I feel better just spending this hour here. What's helped? Just putting it all down and seeing it out there keeps it making sense and shows me I can do it.'

Whatever measure you use, be careful that the person doesn't feel that they and the score are the same thing. Just as the problem is not them, the score is not them either. It's just an indicator of how things are at the moment.

How do you evaluate personal recovery within a large organisation?

We've spent much of our working lives in large NHS Trusts. There is always a tension between using measures that show the impact of a service versus the personal change for a person.

You may well have a service-wide measure that you have to use. That's not a bad thing; it's important to know whether services are effective. How you use them matters.

Be honest with yourself. Do you look at the measure, think with the person you're working with about which elements are most important to them, link the items specifically to the work you're doing and use those bits to help inform what you're doing together? Or do you roll your eyes when you 'hand it' to the person, leave them to 'tick it off' and then put it back in the file without once referring to it in the work you do together?

The problem with the latter is that it's an awful experience for the person and it misses a chance to use the material to support you both. There are no perfect tools but, given that it's likely to be a required part of your organisation in much of the world, there are ways of using them well.

1. The tool itself might very quickly tap into what matters to the person. Brilliant, use it and talk about what it is that the person picks up on in the wording.
2. Most tools ask about a number of things. If there is even just one question that the person is hooked into, take time to think about how you might then measure that in more detail. If it's a question about relationships, work out what elements of relationships matter to them: how often they see people, the number of arguments they have, whether people actively contact them, having a range of friends, having one person to have one shared interest with etc. Then you can create your own mini evaluation that runs alongside the formal one.
3. Keep an eye on the other items in the tool. If you dismiss them early on (maybe you both ridiculed one of the items in the first session), you shut down the chance for the person to later realise and tell you that they do actually matter. Remember that goals change, and people can realise that something else is actually more important than they first thought. Those other items might give you a clue that you need to review what you're working on.
4. Celebrate any changes (without going too 'cheer-leaderly' on them). When you are undergoing significant personal change it can be very easy to look ahead at how much you still want to 'do' and lose sight of how much you've 'done'. It's also our experience that, for some people, it's hard to remember how difficult things were at their worst. That might not be a bad thing and we're not suggesting you revisit that and wallow in it, but the measures can give a quiet reassurance about progress continuing.
5. Use the measure to help you both ride out the dips. The first time progress goes off track can be frightening and emotions such as helplessness can take over. The measures help remind you both that progress was being made (and therefore can be again), that wobbles have happened before (and will do again) and that they're just dips along the way, not an end point.
6. The key point is that, although it can feel as if the evaluation is about feeding some organisational system or proving the worth of the member of staff, finding a way of thinking about progress is really important for the person you are working with.

James' Story

James was a joy with this and we used a combination of percentages and pie charts (for relationships and activities). He had come from brief work with the ward psychologist already talking about the percentage to which he felt recovered. This gave us an immediate way to talk about why he might give himself a different score to that given by other people. And we didn't just use a single score to reflect a week (that would have been unrealistic). We talked about the range of percentages in a week. I was interested in the lows and highs. It mattered that we acknowledged this and even the question about 'what was the lowest score it's been this week' created an expectation that it was okay to talk about the low points as well as the high points – back to the important message that this isn't an exam.

We also had that lovely piece of unexpected evaluation outlined in session 5 when he brought in the drawing we had done previously with himself at the centre and other people positioned around him, gradually further away as their importance to him diminished. We had spent a number of weeks referring to this because the people he cared for were the most important part of his early recovery. One day he brought it in with the 'me' circle in the centre very much enlarged. He beamed and said quite resolutely, 'I've realised I'm important too'. For me, that was the start of James wanting to recover for himself.

Figure 9.1   How James began to describe that he could be as important a focus as other people

We used the relationship chart regularly showing how relationships were developing with the people that mattered to him. The shaded area and the strength of colour were both indications of his progress. It also helped us see when his goals had changed tack and he was able to use the colours to start a conversation about wanting to end a relationship that had previously been very important.

The second chart was about the hobbies and activities that he wanted to pick up. Again it was the dynamic nature of this that mattered. There wasn't a clear progression as he picked up each activity. As we went through work on identity, skills and relationships, it became clear that some of the activities he had originally said he would like to pick up did not fulfil the role he needed and it gave us a route into talking about changing course. We then used these in the outsider witness session to show his daughters how things had developed over time and how his priorities had shifted as his understanding had changed.

Epilogue

I took the draft manuscript to James to see if he was happy with it. His only concern was that people might read the book and think that he had fully recovered and that somehow they ought to do the same. I showed him the lightbulb box in session 1 that talks about 'a life that I'm enjoying' rather than 'recovery' and the comment he had made about being able to write a new chapter in his life. We both agreed that life is full of ups and downs and is never 'sorted'. We just make incremental changes as obstacles arise. Life becomes slightly more enjoyable with each change and, gradually, there is a noticeable overall shift. The eight sessions in this book are just a part of each individual's path to a life that has meaning for them. James still had his folder next to his chair with the exercises in it and still had 'work to do'. But he had also been able to help his nephew who was going through a difficult time because he trusted that James would understand. He had shared his own experiences and been able to give him hope that things would get better.

When we deny the story, it defines us.
When we own the story, we can write a brave new ending.
Brené Brown (2015)

Appendix

Results from the Steps to Recovery Framework

We collected pre and post scores on the Recovery Assessment Scale (RAS), the Warwick-Edinburgh Mental Well-Being Scale (WEMWEBS) and a 9 item self-reported Likert-scale evaluation questionnaire.

The published paper looked at outcomes from 44 participants who had completed the full eight-week STR programme. Thirty-five participants' data could be used for statistical analysis due to data quality issues. There was a medium effect size (d = 0.76) for the pre (42.1±10.9) and post (49.3±7.9) WEMWEBS means and a large effect size (d = 10) for the mean difference from pre (146.4±24.1) and post (163.9±26.3) RAS scores. A Paired 2× Sample t-tests demonstrated a significant increase on post WEMWEBS scores t(34) = −5.8, p<.001, 95% CI [−9.65, −4.64] and post RAS scores t(34) = −7.66, p<.001, 95% CI[−22.13, −12.85]. Both the pre and post WEMWEBS and the RAS variables were significantly strongly positively correlated r(35) = .75, p<.001 and r(35) = .87, p<.001. From the analysis of the evaluation questionnaire, 100% of group participants evaluated the Steps to Recovery Group as having a positive effect on their recovery.

Flaherty-Jones, G.M., Carne, A.S., & Dexter-Smith, S. (2015). The Steps to Recovery Program: Evaluation of a group-based intervention for older individuals receiving mental health services. *Psychiatric Rehabilitation Journal, 39*(1), 68–70.

References

Anthony, W.A. (1993). Recovery from mental illness: The guiding vision of the mental health system in the 1990s. *Innovations and Research, 2*, 17–24.

Brown, B. (2015). Our own history: Change the story. https://brenebrown.com/blog/2015/06/18/own-our-history-change-the-story/

Byron, T. (2015). *The skeleton cupboard: Stories of crisis, sanity and hope*. London: Pan Books.

Carey, M., & Russell, S. (2003). Outsider-witness practices: Some answers to commonly asked questions. *International Journal of Narrative Therapy & Community Work, 1*, 3–16.

Doan, R.E., & Alan, P. (1994). *Story re-visions*. New York: Guilford Press.

Flaherty-Jones, G.M., Carne, A.S., & Dexter-Smith, S. (2015). The Steps to Recovery Program: Evaluation of a group-based intervention for older individuals receiving mental health services. *Psychiatric Rehabilitation Journal, 39*(1), 68–70.

Health and Social Care Information Centre (2018). *Improving access to psychological therapies*. Surrey: Government Statistical Service.

Leamy, M., Bird, V., Le Boutillier, C., Williams, J., & Slade, M. (2011). Conceptual framework for personal recovery in mental health: Systematic review and narrative synthesis. *British Journal of Psychiatry, 199*, 445–52.

Mental Health Foundation (2016). *Relationships in the 21st century: The forgotten foundation of mental health and wellbeing*. London: Mental Health Foundation.

Russo, J., & Sweeney, A. (2016). *Searching for a rose garden: Challenging psychiatry, fostering mad studies*. Monmouth: PCCS Books Ltd.

Smith, K., & Victor, C. (2018). Typologies of loneliness, living alone and social isolation, and their associations with physical and mental health. *Aging and Society*.

Wenzel, A. (2017). *The SAGE encyclopedia of abnormal and clinical psychology*. London: Sage Publications.

White, M., & Epson, D. (1990). *Narrative means to therapeutic ends*. London: W.W. Norton.

Young, S., & Ensing, D. (1999). Exploring recovery from the perspective of people with psychiatric disabilities. *Psychiatric Rehabilitation Journal, 22*(3), 219–231.

Index